BAD vs WORSE

THE ULTIMATE GUIDE
TO MAKING LOSE-LOSE DECISIONS

JOSHUA PIVEN

A PERIGEE BOOK

A PERIGEE BOOK
Published by the Penguin Group
Penguin Group (USA) Inc.
375 Hudson Street, New York, New York 10014, USA
Penguin Group (Canada), 90 Eglinton Avenue East, Suite 700, Toronto, Ontario M4P 2Y3, Canada
(a division of Pearson Penguin Canada Inc.)
Penguin Books Ltd., 80 Strand, London WC2R 0Rl, England
Penguin Group Ireland, 25 St. Stephen's Green, Dublin 2, Ireland (a division of Penguin Books Ltd.)
Penguin Group (Australia), 250 Camberwell Road, Camberwell, Victoria 3124, Australia
(a division of Pearson Australia Group Pty. Ltd.)
Penguin Books India Pvt. Ltd, 11 Community Centre, Panchsheel Park, New Delhi—110 017, India
Penguin Group (NZ), 67 Apollo Drive, Rosedale, North Shore 0632, New Zealand
(a division of Pearson New Zealand Ltd.)
Penguin Books (South Africa) (Pty.) Ltd., 24 Sturdee Avenue, Rosebank, Johannesburg 2196,
South Africa

Penguin Books Ltd., Registered Offices: 80 Strand, London WC2R 0Rl, England

While the author has made every effort to provide accurate telephone numbers and Internet addresses at the time of publication, neither the publisher nor the author assumes any responsibility for
errors, or for changes that occur after publication. Further, the publisher does not have any control
over and does not assume any responsibility for author or third-party websites or their content.

First edition: October 2007

Library of Congress Cataloging-in-Publication Data

Piven, Joshua.
    Bad vs. worse : the ultimate guide to making lose-lose decisions / Joshua Piven.
        p. cm.
    ISBN 978-0-399-53366-2
    1. American wit and humor.   I. Title.   II. Title: Bad versus worse.
    PN6165.P58 2007
    818'.602—dc22

                                                                                2007007592

PRINTED IN THE UNITED STATES OF AMERICA

10 9 8 7 6 5 4 3 2 1

Most Perigee books are available at special quantity discounts for bulk purchases for sales promo-
tions, premiums, fund-raising, or educational use. Special books, or book excerpts, can also be created to fit specific needs. For details, write: Special Markets, Penguin Group (USA) Inc., 375
Hudson Street, New York, New York 10014.

More than any time in history, mankind faces a cross-roads. One path leads to despair and utter hopelessness, the other to total extinction. Let us pray that we have the wisdom to choose correctly.

—Woody Allen

CONTENTS

PART 2: CRITICAL CONDITIONS

PART 3: ARCHVILLAINS

PART 4: KILLER CREATURES

PART 5: PERILOUS PLACES

APPENDIX

Red or white? Window or aisle? Fried or scrambled?

Life is an endless parade of choices, some easy, some more difficult, most minor and inconsequential. Smoking or non? Low-fat or skim? Shave or stubble? These tiny decisions block our path at every turn, each one requiring a few milliseconds of brainpower just so we can go about our daily lives. We choose, then we move on. Every now and then we're faced with a major dilemma, and things get more interesting. Rent or buy? Evolution or creationism? Married or single? Out or in the closet? Burial or cremation?

And then, of course, come the toughest choices of all: the "lose-lose" choices. These are the decisions known as choosing "the lesser of two evils" (or often, in politics, "the evil of two lessers"). It's dire decisions like these that keep people up at night—or at least in the bar for a few more rounds. It's when you'd rather choose "C," but there's only "A" or "B." Essentially, do you cut and run, or stay the course? Either way, and no matter what you do, things are pretty much guaranteed to turn out badly. So, how *do* you make that choice?

That's where this book comes in. *Bad vs. Worse* is the decisive guide to making impossible decisions. It's not a book for people who spend half an hour each morning agonizing over argyle or striped socks. It's not a book for people who must always be the last person at the table to order. Nor is it a book for people who try on ten outfits before choosing one to go out at night. Those people have it easy.

This book is for people who have ever wondered which might be worse, black plague or Spanish flu? Or pondered who would make a better son-in-law, Adolf Hitler or Saddam Hussein? Or tried to decide whether Barry Manilow trumps Neil Diamond in the "most annoying male vocalist over sixty" category. It's the book to have on the coffee table when the discussion moves from "sugar or sweetener?" to "dinner with Charles Manson or Jeffrey Dahmer?" It's the book to have when the renovations are going badly and you wonder who would make a better general contractor, Tony Montana or Tony Soprano? It's the book to have when choosing a summer camp counselor—when that counselor is Dick Cheney or Osama bin Laden.

Bad vs. Worse pairs the world's most evil, deadly, disturbing, and difficult people, places, and things and gives you, the reader, a clear—if extremely difficult—choice: Which one is worser? Ebola or asbestos? Appendicitis or an audit? Tyson or T. rex?

If you've read any of my previous books in *The Worst Case Scenario Survival Handbook* series, you'll be familiar with how to survive various tricky and treacherous situations. This book takes over where those books left off, with the simple premise that when things are bad, they can always get worse. Clearly there's no easy choice when it comes to picking who you'd rather have as a house pet, Jaws or Godzilla. You're probably looking at major medical expenses either way. But as with lots of life's little decisions, there's not always a "correct" answer; you can agonize for hours, but that doesn't necessarily mean you won't regret your decision in the end. History and hindsight have a funny way of making decisions that might once have seemed easy very, very difficult. For example, in 1970 choosing Napoleon or Nixon as your high-school football coach would have been a no-brainer. But what about in late 1973? In 1940, you would probably have chosen a pack of smokes over a pack of wolves any day of the week, and twice on Sunday. What about now? How about ten hours in Baghdad or ten hours in Baltimore?

OK, that last one's never been an easy choice. But the point is, with any difficult quandary you should always make an informed decision. And that's where this book can help. For each impossible choice, you'll find a broad array of possible outcomes, and lots of tips, facts, and background material to help make your decision easier—or harder, as the case may be. For example, you'll be forced to choose between building the pyramids and building the Panama Canal. But before you do, you'll also learn that, while building the pyramids was no doubt seriously hard labor, the workers were probably not slaves and may in fact have been treated better than their modern counterparts in Panama. Plus, no mosquitoes! You'll find out that the cadavers of dead canal workers were sold to medical schools for experiments—and shipped home stuffed in barrels! On the other hand, you'll also learn that ancient Egypt was a feudal society and pyramid workers were essentially born into their lots in life. Don't want to haul stone blocks for the rest of your days? Rather be a chef? Bummer.

You'll also note that, depending on your point of view, some of the choices could reasonably appear in different (or multiple) sections. For example, a good case could be made for Geraldo as an archvillain, or Ozzy at a bar mitzvah as a critical condition. And, really, who would want Richard Nixon as a house pet? For this reason, I've included two helpful sections at the end of the book: a scorecard to help you keep track of your choices, and a list of alternate pairings for you to consider—as well as space to write in your own fantasy bad vs. worse match ups.

Sprinkled throughout the book you'll find additional "choice bits": snippets of trivia and little-known facts you may find helpful in your deliberations, and that may sway your decision. You may find it easier (and more fun) to bring a friend in on the choosing. But which friend? Sorry, can't help you with that one.

So now, go forth and digest, discuss, dispute, and debate. Then carefully consider, because you are the considerer. And then decide.

For you, and only you, are the decider.

—Josh Piven

DANGEROUS PEOPLE

~

WHO WOULD YOU RATHER HAVE AS YOUR BARBER, GENGHIS KHAN OR ATTILA THE HUN?

Two legendary warriors. Two expert swordsmen. One shampoo, condition, and cut. A pair of history's most violent warlords are grinding their shears in anticipation of cutting your throa— er, hair. Try not to squirm as Genghis "The Snipper" Khan and Attila "The Killa" Hun place the smock around your neck, lean the chair back, and ask how much you want taken off the top. The jokes are as stale as their breath, they could both use a manicure, and you're the last client before lunch. But which man has the better sense of style? Which man gives the killer coiffure? It's Mongol vs. Hun in this barber-ian matchup.

He's sometimes known by his given name Temuchin, or variously as Chingis or Jinghis, but you should call him "Sir." After all, Genghis nearly single-handedly united all the disparate, nomadic tribes of Mongolia (the so-called barbarian hordes) into a powerful and ruthless army that terrorized much of Eurasia in the twelfth century. It was a classic clash of civilizations, with the settled agricultural societies of China invaded by the nomads from the steppes of central Asia. And their hair flowed nicely in the breeze.

Genghis's ruthlessness with his enemies is the stuff of legend. It is said that, after defeating the seemingly invincible Tatar armies in battle, he then murdered all remaining men and boys taller than a cart axle. (He called this "trimming some off the top.") His cruelty and killing, however seemingly wanton, always had one goal: consolidating his power by breaking old tribal loyalties that might threaten his reign in the future. As a stylist, his cuts are likely to be shocking and severe, but with purpose. In 1206, with his power at its zenith, Genghis moved out of central Asia and began to terrorize Muslim towns and cities to the west. With his armies mounted on the Mongol pony, Genghis began using siege weapons (catapults, ladders, burning oil) to lay waste to entire population centers, either murdering or enslaving the inhabitants.

But how might Genghis react to criticism of his skills in the beauty parlor? Though there are few definitive records of his personality, it is said that he was a man willing to listen to the opinions of others—though typically he relied only on relatives for advice. He was fond of mixing the carrot and the stick, offering leniency to those who obeyed and abject cruelty to those who didn't. Still, his rules were sometimes applied inconsistently: even armies that surrendered promptly might be slaughtered for tactical or strategic reasons. His powers of persuasion were also said to be formidable, so his suggestions on color, length, and shaping should be weighed carefully. Perhaps most critically, Genghis valued loyalty above all else. If you're considering a new stylist, best to keep quiet about it.

Or Attila?

He's occasionally called Etzel or Atli. In Latin, he's known as *Flagellum Dei*—or "Scourge of God"; it's probably best not to call him "hon." He attacked the Romans, Greeks, and Gauls, and now he's going to attack that unruly mop of split ends.

As a youngster, it is thought that little Attila was taken as a hostage by the Romans, where he learned their civilized ways and customs as well as their political organization. After his release sometime around 434 B.C.E., Attila and his brother Bleda took control of the Hun tribes from their uncle Ruga and negotiated a peace treaty with the Romans. But—and this should be kept in mind when weighing him as a stylist—the Romans didn't pay Attila the agreed-upon sums of gold on time and the Huns began pillaging cities in the eastern Roman provinces. After rampaging through the Balkan peninsula and nearly taking Constantinople—and in the process destroying numerically superior Roman forces—Attila demanded the defeated Romans pay six thousand pounds of gold, and an additional two thousand pounds more each year as tribute. Remember to tip well.

Like Genghis Khan, it's thought that Attila was of Mongoloid origin, though some images give him a more European appearance. His hair was probably worn long, in the barbarian fashion, and washed only rarely. Regardless of his looks, like all Huns Attila was a skilled horseman, often taking meetings, eating, and negotiating treaties from the back of his steed. Attila had a number of children and many descendents and, though he was not a Gaul, some have speculated he and the French king Charlemagne are distantly related. Any such connection would bode well for Attila's fashion sense.

Which man would you want trimming around your ears? Genghis Khan or Attila the Hun, two fierce barbarian warlords ready to lay siege to flaky scalp and frizz, armed for battle with shears, comb, talc, and towel.

G etting sent to the principal's office is bad enough. But what if your punishment included a sit-down with one of history's most strong-willed and uncompromising figures? Get ready to pledge your undying love for communism—or to name names—as you sit in detention, perhaps indefinitely. It's the Great Leap Forward versus the Red Menace in this matchup of Mao Zedong and Senator Joseph McCarthy, two men not especially fond of insolence (and, probably, each other). Hopefully they won't have to call your parents.

As a strict disciplinarian, Mao has little historic competition. By the sheer force of his personality and his iron-fisted control of the Chinese government, Mao is generally held to be responsible for the deaths of tens of millions from famine during the Great Leap Forward, his disastrous drive to industrialize the country. One of his more ill-advised schemes was to scrap China's large steel mills and force peasants to build furnaces and smelters in their backyards. Imagine being sent home with that assignment!

Unfortunately for you, Chairman Mao is likely to be very serious about the power of learning. Mao was born in rural China in 1893 and, though of peasant stock, received a modern education in the Chinese classics. He went on to become a union organizer, but was exiled to the countryside after the communists split with Chiang Kai-shek and the Kuomintang. In exile, he built the Red Army, which went on to take control of mainland China in 1949, and became chairman of the central government council. After what he felt was the Soviet "betrayal" of Marxism—apparently they were just teaching for the tests—Mao led a break with the Russians and the two countries took different paths on the road to communist utopia.

Though clearly an effective bureaucrat, as an educator Mao may have some drawbacks. His experiences during the Cultural Revolution—especially his persecution of, among many other groups, teachers and intellectuals—may not bode well for his patience running an institution of higher learning. On the other hand, he could very well view any classroom high jinks as a positive: trying to play your misbehavior as a rebellion against the "bourgeois" values of high school may be an effective strategy to moderate punishment. If possible, casually drop terms such as "capitalist tool" and "Soviet puppets" during your face-to-face with the chairman. Your teachers are all "Japanese sympathizers, artists, and undesirables." If this strategy doesn't work, consider wearing an "I'm with Mao!" T-shirt.

Or McCarthy?

Red-baiter. Blacklister. Combover-er. But educator? Senator Joseph McCarthy held jobs as a farm hand, grocery store clerk, and usher before leading the Senate's misguided attempt to rid the country of the "scourge" of communism in the 1950s. His unusual educational background indicates he might be a strict disciplinarian as a principal, with little patience for subversive fools (like you). McCarthy attended a one-room schoolhouse in rural Wisconsin in the mid-1910s, but when his parents sent him to a town high school at age nineteen, incredibly he finished a four-year course load in a single year—i.e., he *paid attention*. Thus, he may have little sympathy for six-year seniors and other malcontents.

As the powerful head of the U.S. Senate's Committee on Government Operations and its Permanent Subcommittee on Investigations, McCarthy spent the early 1950s in a relentless, pointless, but nevertheless damaging attempt to uncover communist "infiltrators" and "subversives" both within the government and outside it. He paid particular attention to the arts, where scores of well-known authors, actors, and film directors were called to testify about their own—and, typically, others'—involvement with "anti-American" activities. Some of those called refused to testify, including playwright Arthur Miller and the so-called Hollywood Ten, and were jailed for contempt. Others, fearful of being blacklisted and thus unable to work, named names. These controversial figures, notably Elia Kazan, cofounder of the Actors' Studio and director of *On the Waterfront*, were disgraced and remain lightning rods of discussion to this day. McCarthy was later discovered to have lied repeatedly during his career, and to have accepted money from communist-controlled unions during his election campaign. So, if all else fails, try to bribe your way out of trouble.

Think long and hard before taking "the Fifth" in Principal McCarthy's office. Trained as a lawyer and judge, "Tail-gunner Joe" is an expert in the black art of twisting innocuous-seeming statements into admission of guilt. For example, phrases such as "I needed to go to the bathroom" could be interpreted as "Stalin rules!" Do not even consider postulating that you were "acting alone" when you fired the spitball at the teacher. McCarthy is likely to see such an explanation as a blatant attempt to cover up a "vast conspiracy" of "left-wing" spitballers seeking to "overthrow the educational system as we know it." Your response to questions such as "Are you now or have you ever been a student at this school?" should not be answered with "Can you define *student*?" or "Can you repeat the question?" or "You'll be purged and this school will be collectivized when we communists take over the United States." On the other hand, you may be able to escape punishment if you're willing to sell your soul and accuse your fellow students of any conceivable transgression, however minor. Be aware that if you ask Principal McCarthy if he has "no sense of decency, sir?" you may be in for trouble.

Who would you rather have making that all-important phone call home, Mao or McCarthy? Regardless, don't forget your ace in the hole: branding your teachers bourgeoisie should work in either case.

Are you ready for some . . . tyraaaannnnts? OK, not tyrants exactly, but controversial leaders whose prowess in foreign policy was sometimes overshadowed by domestic, er, indiscretions. Both men had extremely loyal followings and led their respective countries during periods of great social upheaval. Both were seen as saviors by some, power-hungry plagues upon the populace by others. And both ended their careers in exile. But the real test for any leader is (or should be, anyway) how well he can motivate a squad of unruly seventeen-year-olds on the football field. It's a position that requires tactical skill, a keen understanding of one's opponents, and great secrecy. In other words, it's Waterloo vs. Watergate in this coaching contest.

Yes, he was short—though not as short as you might think: he was really five feet, six and a half inches, in his day actually slightly taller than average. But his outsized tactical acumen and strategic prowess as a general and politician dwarf any physical shortcomings. (He was also typically surrounded by very tall guards, making him appear shorter than he was; he should feel right at home in the locker room.) Might his unique set of skills translate to victory on the gridiron?

Napoleon was a rising star in the French military, commanding an artillery unit fighting against the royalists and the British in Toulon by the time he was promoted to brigadier general late in 1793 at age twenty-four. Through political connections, as well as the successful destruction of the rebellious royalists in Paris in 1795, Napoleon became commander of the Army of the Interior ("Go Army! Beat Navy!"). He went on to command the Army of Italy, which went on to take Turin and occupy Milan. He was, however, as much a political leader as a military one. He created a Jacobin republic in Lombardy, modeled after the French Republic, which he eventually merged with Modena and Bologna, creating the Italian Republic and, later, the Kingdom of Italy.

Due to his enormous success as a general, as a football coach Napoleon would command respect from his own players as well as the opposing players and coaches. He was, however, not invincible. Napoleon was smart enough to recognize his own army's weaknesses (no offensive line), including the inferiority of the French navy. Rather than attack Britain outright and risk a disaster at the hands of the British fleet, he attempted to cut off supply routes (an "end around") by invading and occupying Egypt. This plan proved disastrous, however, and led to an alliance of Britain, Austria, Russia, and Turkey against France. After Napoleon was ultimately defeated at Waterloo, he was sent into exile on St. Helena, a barren volcanic isle in the South Atlantic, where he wrote his memoirs before his death in 1821 (either of stomach cancer or accidental poisoning).

Though there is little historical evidence to support it, it is thought that Napoleon's habit of "running up the casualties" during lopsided military victories—as well as his penchant for "trash-talking" about opposing generals—may have helped embolden his enemies. Further, his odd sense of personal style (he had a crew cut and was known as *le petit tondou*, or "little crop head") made him the butt of on-battlefield jokes. And he was less than fond of having a cask of wine dumped over his head after victories.

Commanding men to victory is certainly one of Napoleon's strong suits, and would likely translate to some success on the field. He was, however, excessively fond of treaties, a disposition which may lead to the surrender of critical games as part of an overall strategy to dominate high school football and, through it, all of sport. Additionally, he is almost certain to appoint himself first consul as well as coach, giving him control of day-to-day team operations, staffing, draft picks, magistrates, trainers, judges, civil servants, and the guys who do all the laundry. All in the service of victory, of course.

Or Nixon?

Expect lots of "dirty trick" plays with Dick Nixon at the helm, guiding the squad to victory after victory—especially if that entails breaking into the opposing team's locker room and stealing their playbook. With assistant coach Henry "Bubba" Kissinger at his side, Nixon and his cadre of loyalists will no doubt whip the team into shape, verbally attacking all stragglers as "communist spies," "sissies," and "Democrats."

Like Napoleon, Nixon was a military man: he rose to the rank of Lieutenant Commander in the Navy during World War II before rejoining civilian life and successfully running for the House of Representatives in 1946. In his role on the infamous House Un-American Activities Committee, Nixon was instrumental in the conviction of Alger Hiss for perjury. Yes, apparently Nixon was an absolute *stickler* about honesty, but on the sidelines you may be more concerned with his foul mouth, ill temper, and racist rants. During his run for the U.S. Senate in 1950, Nixon was tagged with the epithet "Tricky Dick" for his ruthless attacks against his opponent, about whom he distributed "pink sheets" comparing her voting record to that of a supposed communist.

Of course, Nixon could also be surprisingly modest and forthcoming, albeit in a calculated way. During his famous Checkers speech, he acknowledged running a "slush fund" filled with political contributions from well-connected businessmen, though at the same time denied the money was used for illegal activity. (He never admitted to taking money from booster clubs or alums, however.) He noted that his daughter's "mascot," a spaniel named Checkers, was also a political gift, but added that "we are going to keep it." The speech was a huge success and led Dwight Eisenhower to offer Nixon the vice-presidential spot on the Republican presidential ticket in 1952. Nixon served two terms as vice president and was later elected president—before resigning in disgrace in 1974.

Nixon's various qualities and successes as a politician and peacemaker—attempts to understand foreign peoples and cultures, support for arms reduction, and affirmative action—tend to be overshadowed (perhaps rightly) by his paranoia and anticommunist fervor. How might such traits translate to his coaching acumen? Nixon inspires manic loyalty, a good quality in a high school coach. Unfortunately this loyalty often results in illegal activity, be it breaking into a hotel or meddling in the affairs of foreign governments. Whether wearing a "good cloth coat" or not, Nixon is likely to sweat profusely on the sidelines, perhaps tipping off opponents when a trick play is in the offing. On the other hand, Nixon's coaching staff (his "plumbers") may have some success planting stories in the local media discrediting opposing coaches and players. Conversely, it's best to be wary of letting reporters into your team's pregame meetings, lest dogged journalists get a line on game-day decisions from their informant "Go Deep Throat." And, on occasion, eighteen-and-a-half minutes of game tape may disappear.

Napoleon had a crew cut, Nixon a five o'clock shadow. Two leaders fond of treaties but at the same time hungry for power, two military men who mercilessly attacked their enemies yet ulti-

 **CHOICE BITS**

* While living in exile, Napoleon refused to ride "within sight" of his British captors, calling it "offensive."

* Napoleon, never royalty, demanded to be called "Your Majesty" by his British minders; instead they called him "General Bonaparte."

* Nixon was pardoned by President Ford in 1974 for "all offenses" beginning January 20, 1969—the day Nixon was inaugurated.

* In a meeting with his congressional supporters just before his resignation speech, Nixon broke down and cried (shades of Dick Vermeil?).

mately landed in exile. It's third and long, under two minutes to go. Crunch time. Who will get the Gatorade shower? You make the call.

It's going to be a glorious June wedding: bright sunshine, a New England B&B with a white picket fence, fragrant floral arrangements, and open bar. The vows will tug at your heartstrings, the honeymoon will be in Greece, and your baby—your only daughter—is simply radiant in a white gown. There's only one thing that could spoil this picture postcard of a day, and that's the groom from hell: Adolf or Saddam. They're both vying for her hand, they've come to ask your permission, and they've got the *Wehrmacht* and the Republican Guard, respectively, backing them up. Which of the twentieth century's worst dictators gets the nod?

An artist at heart, Hitler could offer a potential mate a creative outlook on life—though his failure to pass the entrance exam for the Vienna Academy of Fine Arts may preclude the arts as a career choice. Hitler—he insists on being called "son" or *Führer* (dad)—has great rhetorical skill and is readily able to make a convincing argument for why he's the best choice for your daughter's hand. His monologues, however, tend to go on for hours, and may be punctuated by occasional hand slamming, showers of spittle, and calls to arms. It's worth considering his love of animals (the nonhuman kind, that is) as a major plus, and he dotes on his dog, a German shepherd (what else?) named Blondi. As a husband, he'd provide your daughter with a number of well-equipped and well-guarded homes and highly secure *Führerbunkers* as well as the famed *Berchtesgaden*, a mountain retreat in Bavaria. His wine and art collections are said to be vast, collected from all over Europe—and even Russia!

There are of course a few negatives. The pathological paranoia; constant chatter about some sort of a *blitzkrieg* attack on Europe; a possibly ill-timed invasion of the Soviet Union, and the virulent anti-Semitism could make for awkward dinner table conversation. And Hitler is almost certain to object to a big Jewish wedding. (The *chuppah* could be out, for now.) Personality-wise, *Der Führer* tends to fall on the dictatorial side of bossy, and presumably he would expect his orders to be carried out to the letter. What's more, potential grandchildren might be confused by all the sub-*führers*, the *sturmbahnführers* and the *untersturmbahnführers* and the *Hitlerjugendführers*—all of them jockeying for control, arguing over who's in charge. Picking ushers could lead to some sort of international incident.

Also, and there's no getting around it, Adolf is definitely on the shorter side. And the food caught in the little moustache? Could be embarrassing during the soup course. All in all, you think your daughter might be able to do better.

Or Hussein?

But *Saddam*? Or possibly it's pronounced "*Sadd*-am." Or "*Sad-dam*." No one seems to know for sure, and he's not given to straight answers. There's no denying it, the man certainly has charm—unless it's one of his doubles who's been rather chatty. Of course, all the doppelgängers could be a real bonus around the house, taking out the trash, picking up the kids from school, and getting dinner on the table. But there may be a bit of fat that needs trimming: Does each double really *need* a palace, a man-made lake, and a fleet of Rolls-Royces? On the other hand, easy access to five-cents-per-gallon gas is likely to make driving across the desert at a moment's notice very affordable.

Money aside, Saddam does appear to have a stable of important friends—lifelong allies like Donald Rumsfeld could conceivably drop in for coffee. Admittedly, though, the man's environmental responsibility is pretty suspect: draining the marshes, setting the oil wells on fire, and releasing poison gas don't point to a real "greenie." There could be more than a few global warming arguments over breakfast.

The weapons of mass destruction, too, are a bit worrisome. If they exist. Again, no one seems to have a straight answer. Saddam tends to brag about them, and the Scud missiles are indeed worrisome. But it's just quite possible that he's a very good bluffer—best to avoid playing poker with the man! There is another troubling thing, though. Saddam might have been married before. Perhaps to multiple wives. Of course, polygamy is accepted in many cultures. But your daughter may have other ideas, and it could present a problem during the wedding ceremony—"harem" has such a negative connotation these days. (Saddam's also been pretty clear on the "no Kurds in the wedding party" rule.) The firing of the AK-47s into the ceiling during the reception is not likely to go over well with the hotel, either. It could mean losing your deposit.

The wedding cake promises to be super, however. From the three-foot swimming pool carved out of buttercream and filled with champagne to the huge bust of the man himself perched atop the roof, a wedding cake made to resemble a forty-room Greek Revival–style palace is really something. And with a working elevator! But his neglect in putting a likeness of your daughter on the cake could be a sign of excessive ego, something to watch for. Saddam's sons seem likable enough, and well dressed. They appear to be major car collectors, and hobbies are good. But that Uday seems a bit of a playboy. Saddam may give him too long a leash.

So, who's it going to be? Hitler or Hussein? It's a tough call. At least Hussein is a general. Hitler's only a corporal. Doesn't that mean Hussein has a better pension?

Two middle-class women, both attractive, well educated, and with a penchant for sharp-edged cutting tools. Of course, Lizzie Borden is (allegedly) one of the most notorious killers of all time, while Lorena Bobbitt wielded her blade with more precision but presumably less murderous intent. But then again, Lizzie was an animal lover and was never convicted, and Lorena, well, her fingerprints were all over the evidence. It's the ultimate in nightmare girlfriend matchups, Lizzie versus Lorena, two ladies with major grudges and axes to grind. But you have no choice; you can't date both at the same time. One of them's got to go. But which one? Whomever you choose, try to let her down easy.

Lizzie Borden took an axe
And gave her mother forty whacks.
And when she saw what she had done,
She gave her father forty-one.

—Children's nursery rhyme

The actual number of blows was more like nineteen for her mother (actually stepmother) and eleven for Lizzie's father—children tend to exaggerate when singing about premeditated capital murder. But the result was nevertheless the same in one of the most celebrated criminal cases of all time, the O. J. Simpson trial of the nineteenth century (and like O.J., she got off). Lizzie, an unmarried churchgoer and Sunday-school teacher, is the attractive daughter of one of the richest men in Fall River, Massachusetts. Never especially close to Abby, her stepmother (she was killed first), Lizzie is nevertheless a loving daughter and also very close to her sister, Emma, also unmarried. How might Lizzie react when faced with the distressing news that you're calling off the romance? At the inquest, she was accused of buying prussic acid and attempting to poison her father and stepmother—charges that were never heard at trial due to a technicality. But nevertheless, breaking the news while eating out instead of eating at home may be the way to go.

On the other hand, Lizzie is a good dresser and fastidious about her appearance, to the point of burning a set of clothes just after the murder—clothes she claimed were soiled with "paint."

And, of course, there's the not-insignificant fact that no murder weapon was ever found and Lizzie had no traces of blood on her body. Both point to her innocence of the crime. Then there's the question of motive. There was some evidence that Lizzie's father was planning to draw up a new will, a will that would leave the bulk of his half-million-dollar estate ($10 million in today's dollars) to his second wife, leaving Lizzie and her sister just $25,000 each. And Lizzie's sister was out of the house during the period the murders took place. She had motive, and opportunity.

Jilting Lizzie could also have significant legal ramifications, should she choose to sue. Her defense lawyers were among the most skilled in the state, and her legal team managed to convince the judges to rule all of Lizzie's incriminating statements, made during the inquest, inadmissible. Her lawyers also succeeded in finding witnesses who testified to the presence of a "strange man" hanging around the Borden home on the fateful morning of August 4, 1892. As in the O.J. case, this "mysterious stranger" was never found.

Or Lorena?

Behind bedroom door number two lurks five-foot, two-inch Lorena L. Bobbitt, kitchen knife at the ready. Unlike Lizzie, Lorena readily admitted to her crime: she was guilty, but with an explanation. Also unlike Lizzie, in court she took the stand in her own defense, explaining helpfully that "the refrigerator door was open, and that was the only light. And I turned and saw the knife. I took it. I went to the bedroom. I pulled the sheets off, and I cut him." Specifically, she performed an emergency "penectomy," without anesthetic. (Penectomy is similar to castration, but a cut above.) Shortly thereafter she left the scene of the crime, getting in her car and throwing the evidence out the window. (It was later recovered and surgically reattached.)

Lorena, who was charged with "malicious wounding" in the 1993 trial and faced twenty years in prison, claimed her husband had abused her repeatedly. John Wayne Bobbitt's lawyer, on the other hand, portrayed Lorena as a social climber who wanted to hurt her husband, a selfish lover. (Though, as even his own lawyer later admitted, Bobbitt "may not be the most sensitive lover there is.") But was she telling the truth about the abuse? Lorena had admitted to the police that her husband did not satisfy her sexually, complicating her claim of marital sexual abuse. Eventually, both John Wayne and Lorena Bobbitt were acquitted at trial, prompting late-night comedians to note that "the evidence didn't stand up in court." You might want to think twice about

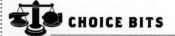 **CHOICE BITS**

* In 1997, a jury of Stanford Law School alumni, faculty, and students, in a mock Borden trial presided over by Supreme Court Justices William Rehnquist and Sandra Day O'Connor, found Lizzie Borden not guilty of the axe murders.

* John Wayne Bobbitt was arrested again in 1994, this time for allegedly attacking his fiancée, a former topless dancer.

* Bobbitt's penis was successfully surgically reattached, and he later appeared in two porn videos: *Uncut* and *Frankenpenis*.

jilting Lorena, as you could be embroiled in years of costly legal wrangling and a number of expensive and painful surgeries. And then of course there is likely to be a lifetime of socially awkward pauses when anyone mentions chopping, cutting, slicing, filleting, deboning, removing the skin, taking some off the top, or shortening anything.

Keeping all the facts of the cases in mind, who would you rather jilt, Lizzie or Lorena? Put a different way, if you had to pick one woman, who would you rather have as a girlfriend (or wife), Lorena or Lizzie? Either way, sleeping with one eye open is not a bad idea.

The grill is piping hot, a hearty, full-bodied cabernet is in the decanter, and the candles are throwing complicated shadows on the dining room wall. Two large flank steaks, charred on the outside but a deep shade of purple-crimson in the center, lay waiting on a serving platter, their juices nearly running onto the counter. Everything is as it should be for an intimate dinner at home with . . . one of the most dangerous and disturbed serial killers of all time! It's charisma versus cannibalism in this macabre matchup, and you've got to pick which man you'd rather spend an evening—or however long you survive—with.

I am what you have made me and the mad dog devil killer fiend leper is a reflection of your society . . . Whatever the outcome of this madness that you call a fair trial or Christian justice, you can know this: In my mind's eye my thoughts light fires in your cities.

—Statement by Charles Manson upon his sentencing

So, he's not precisely remorseful. But Manson does have a way with words. Might he not make an interesting dinner companion? After all, a bad dinner is always a good story later, right? Charles Manson was born in 1934 to an alcoholic mother who was sentenced to prison for robbery when her son was just five. Young Charlie was sent to—and escaped from—various reform schools for crimes such as burglary, armed robbery, and car theft. By the early 1960s, he had fathered two children and become a pimp in Southern California. After being sentenced to ten years in federal prison for violating the terms of his probation, he learned to play guitar and began writing music; he claimed he wanted to become a songwriter after his release. He also claimed to be a Scientologist (and you thought Tom Cruise was odd!).

On August 8, 1969, Manson convinced four of his followers to break into the home of actress Sharon Tate, where he had had a prior run-in some months before. Manson's followers broke into the home, stabbing Tate and four others to death. Manson had told his "family" that "now is the time for Helter Skelter." The killing spree continued the following day, claiming two more victims. Manson was convicted of first-degree murder and sentenced to death in April 1971. After California outlawed the death penalty, Manson's sentence was changed to life in prison. He has been denied parole ten times, and continues to dine on prison fare.

But how might Charlie Manson behave at the dinner table? Manson was obsessed with the Beatles' *White Album*, which could offer fertile ground for discussion and conversations about music (avoid mentioning songs like "Helter Skelter" and "Happiness Is a Warm Gun," however). Perhaps he might offer to serenade you with "Cry Baby Cry" or "Everybody's Got Something to Hide Except for Me and My Monkey." Manson also had his own rather unusual interpretation of the book of Revelation, which could spawn discourse on the bible. Specifically, he saw himself as "the fifth angel" who would be given "the key to the pit of the abyss." Revelation 9:3 says that "out of the smoke came forth locusts upon the earth"; Manson felt these locusts were in fact "beetles," i.e., Beatles. Best to stay away from the subject of insects altogether.

There is one minor complication to a steak dinner with Manson. It's a small point, but Manson reportedly interpreted Revelation 9:4 ("And it was said unto them that they should not hurt the grass of the earth, neither any green thing, neither any tree, but only such men as have not the seal of God on their foreheads") as a stricture not to kill any living thing (save man). Thus, putting freshly carved flank steak in front of Manson may result in unforeseen and undesired consequences.

Confessed killer, cannibal, boiler of skulls. But there was more to Jeffrey Dahmer than murderous rage and insanity. He reportedly enjoyed spending time at the mall, working in a candy factory (he was laid off), and storing his victim's hearts in the freezer ("to eat later"). Would a quiet dinner with Dahmer *necessarily* end badly? It all depends if he decides to have you for dessert.

Dahmer first killed in 1978, the victim a hitchhiker he picked up in an Ohio suburb. After a stint as an orderly in the military—where, though never proven, it's suspected Dahmer killed on or near an Army base in West Germany—Dahmer found work in a chocolate factory. (Whether he had a sweet tooth is unknown, but best to keep a dessert on hand.) Dahmer was a homosexual who picked up his victims with promises of money and beer in exchange for posing nude for photographs. He was convicted of molesting a boy in 1989, though he served just ten months in prison. After his release, his inner beast ran amok and he proceeded to lure, drug, and kill sixteen men and boys, eating parts of some victims and using a fifty-five-gallon drum to destroy the remains with acid. At trial, Dahmer's own attorney described his client as "a very sick young man." You don't say!

But Dahmer also had a mischievous streak and an offbeat sense of humor. He snuck into a photograph of his high school honor society even though his grades were middling; a photo editor blacked out his face before the yearbook went to print. (He did it again a year later.) He nipped at a bottle of Scotch during class. On a school trip to Washington, D.C., he managed to talk his way into Walter Mondale's office. But he was not exactly a normal kid.

* Sharon Tate was the wife of film director Roman Polanski.

* Manson believed the door to paradise was in a cave somewhere in Death Valley, California.

* The Manson crime scenes included his "teachings," scrawled in blood on the walls.

* Dahmer came from a broken home.

* Dahmer worked for the Ambrosia Chocolate Co., which made bulk chocolate for many companies, including Hostess and Pillsbury.

Neighbors reported seeing small animal burial grounds next to his house; he kept squirrel skeletons in jars. He liked to drink, a habit which eventually led to his discharge from the Army. When he became drunk, his eyes would glaze over and his face would become devoid of emotion, like "he just wasn't there," according to a man who knew him.

If Dahmer came over for dinner, you might consider keeping the cork in the wine, lest his demons be released. (And, since he tended to slip his victims Mickeys, this would also be an act of self-preservation.) It's clear that Dahmer enjoyed eating meat, though it's not known for certain if he favored beef as well as human flesh. But he once admitted to frying a victim's bicep in shortening and eating it, so chances are good he's not overly particular about his diet.

Who, then, is coming to dinner? Though clearly insane, Manson might be a better conversationalist, as Dahmer tended to travel on the fringes of society, while Manson was at least moderately cultured. On the other hand, Dahmer was a photography buff and knew a bit about cooking.

The Torah service is over, the rabbi and cantor are relaxing with a glass of Manischewitz, and, on your instructions, your ninety-year-old mother-in-law has turned her hearing aid way up. It's time to party, to celebrate your son's entrance into manhood. All his friends are gathered around the stage, waiting for the band. The curtain rises and a shadow moves across the wall. A figure, long-haired and dressed in black, approaches the mic. You double check, and it's not the rabbi. It's either Ozzy "The Prince of Darkness" Osbourne or Marilyn "Charlie" Manson— your choice in this epic battle of heavy metal heavyweights. But who will it be? And which one does a better rendition of Kool and the Gang's "Celebration"?

He's been known to bite the heads off bats on stage. He's covered in crucifix tattoos. He's barely intelligible. And his first group was Black Sabbath—perhaps not the reference you're looking for at the megamitzvah. His album titles include *Diary of a Madman*, *The Ultimate Sin*, and *No Rest for the Wicked*. Still, Ozzy has an enormous following among teens, and his appearance could make your party the hit of the mitzvah season. Just don't ask him to recite the Kaddish.

Ozzy has sold tens of millions of records, both as a solo artist and with Black Sabbath, the band he fronted until 1979. He never finished high school, though, so he's not exactly a role model for a thirteen-year-old. And there are other wrinkles. As a youngster, Ozzy was in and out of jail around Birmingham, England, incarcerated for various crimes including burglary and theft—he reportedly once broke into a building wearing gloves with the fingers cut off (hey, he never claimed to be a genius). He was arrested soon after. He also punched a police officer.

However, Ozzy is a devoted husband and father and has encouraged his children to pursue careers in music and acting; his wife, Sharon, is also his manager. Still, controversy has swirled around the rocker for decades, beginning with his biting the head off a bat during a concert; Ozzy later was said to quip that he "had to get rabies shots, but the bat had to get Ozzy shots." It's rumored that he also bit the head off a dove during a meeting with record executives, and he was arrested for urinating on the Alamo. The messages behind Ozzy's music are also somewhat controversial. For example, the singer was sued by the parents of a teen who killed himself because, they claimed, their son listened to the rocker's song "Suicide Solution" once too often. The case was dismissed. (Consider asking the Prince of Darkness to remove this song from his bar mitzvah repertoire, however.) Another tune, "Bark at the Moon," supposedly led to a stabbing: A Canadian teen testified in court that his friend Jimmy "said that every time he listened to the song he felt strange inside. He said when he heard it on New Year's Eve he went out and stabbed someone."

On the other hand, Ozzy has always been a huge Beatles fan, and sometimes listens to the Fab Four before going on stage. Depending on his mood, it may be worth requesting a cover ("Hey Jude"?) to really get the older folks moving on the dance floor.

There's no getting around the fact that Ozzy's music tends to be on the louder side—after all, he's used to playing stadiums. Consider booking a room slightly larger than the downstairs social hall at the synagogue. The music tends to be fast, with lots of screeching guitars and shouting, and a mosh pit is almost certain to develop in front of the stage. Older guests and those with canes and walkers should probably be seated near the back.

Or Marilyn?

He dresses in black, wears white face paint with black eye makeup, and looks like Howard Stern on a really bad day. He's fond of blood, crucifixes, skulls, knives, and gothic typography that looks suspiciously of Germanic origin. And his latest tour is "Against All Gods." But does that include Adonai?

Marilyn Manson (his real name is the more prosaic Brian Warner) certainly doesn't shy away from controversy, and there's no telling what he'll do on stage during the bar mitzvah. Performing in Utah, he once ripped apart the Book of Mormon, outraging Mormons around the world. (Best to keep the Torah scrolls tucked away.) Like Ozzy's, his album names tend to strike an unsettling chord, with titles like *Antichrist Superstar* and *Smells Like Children*. Unlike Ozzy, however, Manson's entire schtick—including his music—has been tagged as phony, a made-up, well-marketed-but-meaningless Goth ghoul image intended only to appeal to disaffected suburban teenagers and take their money. In other words, he could be a major hit!

Warner was a music journalist before he was discovered in Florida by Trent Reznor of Nine Inch Nails (and the similarities between the two are hard to miss). Reznor backed Warner's band, and the young man from Ohio took on the "Marilyn Manson" moniker, a combination of Marilyn Monroe and Charles Manson (though Warner looks like neither). Like Ozzy—some might claim intentionally so—Manson created buzz wherever he appeared, particularly during one concert in July 2001, where he reportedly urinated on a security guard from the stage. He was later charged with criminal sexual misconduct. A few months later, a different security guard alleged that Manson rubbed his genitals on the man's head. Events such as these may suggest hiring a small security detail for the mitzvah. Consider providing them with wide-brimmed hats and rain gear.

While his true religious views are murky, Manson is fortunately involved in some form of worship. In fact, he's an ordained minister: in the 1990s Manson was officially given the title of "reverend" in the Church of Satan by Anton LaVey, the church's

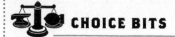

CHOICE BITS

* After he bit the head off the bat, Ozzy's concerts were boycotted by the Humane Society.

* An ad for Ozzy's first band read, "Black Sabbath makes Led Zeppelin look like a kindergarten house band."

* Marilyn Manson was once married to a burlesque dancer, stage name "Dita Von Teese."

founder. Many critics have questioned his musical talent (as well as his sanity), but Manson has some acumen both as a painter and an author. Time permitting, during a break in the show you might consider asking him to sign copies of his bestselling autobiography, *The Long Hard Road Out of Hell*.

Who, then, will take the stage after prayers have been intoned and the *ruggalah* have been eaten? Will it be the Prince of Darkness himself, or Satan's reverend? Whomever you choose, *mazel tov!*

You've filled the tank (or at least put in as much gas as you can afford), chilled the water bottles, and checked the oil. The sun is shining, the tires have good pressure, and the kids aren't fighting—yet. You're ready to hit the road, and everything's perfect. Well, not exactly perfect. There's one small problem with the music selection. Your satellite radio is malfunctioning and it only gets two channels, and you've got to pick one: twenty-four hours of Manilow or twenty-four hours of Diamond. And there seems to be an electrical glitch in the system preventing you from turning the radio off, or the volume down. So, you're faced with a choice: "Copacabana" or "Cracklin' Rosie"? Over and over and over. Across several states. But which "showman" to choose? Removing the battery is not an option. Neither is running the car off the road.

There's no denying his success: the man has sold sixty-five million records. But there is some denying his talent. Dismissed by critics as a master of schlocky, overproduced fluff for the adult contemporary market, Manilow gets little respect as a performer, though some credit him with acceptable songwriting chops—even though his famous tune "I Write the Songs (That Make the Whole World Sing)" was written by someone else. But few performers have dominated their niche like Barry, a man with more than a dozen number-one hits on the adult contemporary charts. The evidence? We all know the words to such four-minute sapfests as "Can't Smile Without You," "Looks Like We Made It," and "Even Now." Is it legal to drive wearing ear muffs?

Barry Manilow (real name Barry Alan Pincus; Manilow is his mother's maiden name) attended Julliard while working in the mailroom at CBS. But he got his big break in the early 1970s when Bette Midler, then an unknown lounge singer, hired him as her pianist and musical director. Midler's famous "gay bathhouse" tour in New York led to some exposure (not that kind!), and Manilow was given a small recording contract with Bell Records (later Arista). His first album flopped, but with his release of a rearranged UK hit called "Brandy"—Manilow changed the name to "Mandy"—he was off. An amazing run of twenty-five consecutive Top 40 adult contemporary hits followed, including such showstoppers as "Even Now" and, of course, "Copacabana," one of his few up-tempo numbers. At one point, *Rolling Stone* magazine's "Showman of Our Generation" (*whose* generation?) had

43

DANGEROUS PEOPLE

five albums charting at once, up to that time a feat accomplished by only Johnny Mathis and Frank Sinatra. Manilow even won an Emmy award for 1977's *Barry Manilow Special*, an ABC program that attracted an astonishing thirty-seven million viewers (no record on how many were asleep after the opener).

The problem, of course, is the music. It's *boring*. Not only that, it's boring and hard to turn off, because it's familiar. What's more, while listening to, say, James Taylor connotes a certain respect for a '60s icon whose music had a message, listening to Manilow is just not socially acceptable in any context, save in a retirement home. Imagine leaving your Manilow LPs lying around the house for your friends to see. Or an "all Manilow" dinner party. For some unknowable reason, Manilow is not even accorded the same ironic, knowing respect as his contemporaries The Bee Gees. He's just, well, Barry Manilow. Irony need not apply.

Could you listen to "This One's for You," "Tryin' to Get the Feeling Again," "Daybreak," and "(Why Don't We Try) A Slow Dance" for fifteen hours straight? What if the station, in a fiendish mood, decided to play and play and replay his 1998 album *Manilow Sings Sinatra*? Could you make it through? Perhaps a Manilow-only morning commute, or a few songs while driving over (or off) a bridge. But *fifteen hours*? At least there wouldn't be too many repeats: Manilow has forty-four albums. Gulp.

Or Diamond?

Remember The Monkees' "I'm a Believer"? The song hit number one on the *Billboard* Hot 100 chart in December 1966. It was later used in the movie *Shrek*, recorded by Smash Mouth. That song was written by none other than Neil Diamond, though it didn't do nearly as well when Diamond released it on his own *September Morn* album years after The Monkees made it a hit. But that's how it's gone for Diamond: his songs have been recorded by numerous bands over the years, he's sold millions of records, and he still gets no respect.

How come? Maybe it's the rhinestone-studded costumes. Or the tight pants. Or all that luxurious chest hair. Perhaps it's that Neil Diamond, like Manilow, has always been a sex symbol—to postmenopausal women. Few people under age sixty take him seriously, and yet somehow we all know his songs: "Cracklin' Rosie," "Song Sung Blue," "Touching You, Touching Me," "Sweet Caroline," and *ET*'s tear-jerker "Turn On Your Heartlight." But somehow, someway, he's sold more than hundred million albums. And for fifteen hours, you're going to listen to every one of them. Twice.

Like Manilow, Neil Diamond (his real name) grew up in New York—and even attended school with Barbra Streisand and Neil Sedaka. He attended New York University on, of all things, a fencing scholarship, but later dropped out to become a full-time songwriter. He signed a $5 million deal with Columbia Records in 1971 and two years later released *Jonathan Livingston Seagull* which went multiplatinum. Other hits followed, including the now-legendary *Jazz Singer* soundtrack in 1980, which went quintuple platinum and rocketed Diamond to fame with the painfully boring lullaby "Hello Again" and the rollickin' "Acapulco" and more soulful "America." Diamond went on to release gold single after gold single, through the 1980s and '90s. Even his brief detour into country music with 1996's *Tennessee Moon* was a success, with the album improbably reaching number three on the country charts. His latest album, *12 Songs*, was a critical and commercial success, and even *Rolling Stone* magazine, that hippist-of-the-hip arbiter of musical taste, named the album's single "Evermore" number one on its "Top Ten Tracks" list. Could the sixty-six-year-old showman actually be hip?

No.

Nevertheless, everything the man touches, it seems, turns to gold—or platinum. It would probably not be too difficult to spend fifteen hours just listening to Diamond songs that have charted, much less his entire catalog. Nevertheless—and even though the postmodern ironic band Phish covered "Cracklin' Rosie"—his songs are still mostly melancholy mush pumped up with fancy orchestral arrangements. And oh, those outfits.

So which near-septuagenarian, Barry or Neil, gets to sing you to sleep while you're behind the wheel? It's a serious problem, choosing between "Copacabana" and "Acapulco," but you've got to make the call. Just do your family a favor and have them take a separate car.

PART TWO

CRITICAL CONDITIONS

A visit to the dentist's chair isn't most people's idea of a good time. Only masochists (and perhaps other dentists) look forward to a few hours of having their teeth drilled. But what if the dentist's drill was the least of your worries? What if, twenty minutes after leaning back in the chair, you noticed something odd, something *just not right*, on your dentist's hand? (Oh, and he's not wearing gloves. Latex allergy.) Could it be . . . ? Might it be . . . ? Yes, Jim, it looks like either *necrotizing fasciitis* or leprosy! Yikes. But which one is it? And which one would you *rather* it be? Time to choose your highly transmissible skin condition. Oh, and it looks like you need a root canal, too.

It's a bacteria seemingly designed for the information age: it spreads easily, attacks nearly overnight, is extremely painful and gross to look at, and can cause death if left untreated. You may not be fond of your dentist—isn't that what their spouses are for?—but it's not something you would wish on anybody. And it's surely not something you want anywhere near your mouth.

Necrotizing fasciitis is a rare bacterial infection that destroys skin cells, fat, and the tissue that covers muscle. It is a very serious infection with a mortality rate of about 30 percent and, perhaps even more frightening, it often infects otherwise healthy people, generally via a cut or abrasion in the skin (though not always: it can occur in areas where the skin is not broken). The bacterium that causes the condition varies, but the most typical is group A streptococcal, the same bacterium that causes strep throat. The term *flesh-eating* is not precisely accurate: the bacterium works quickly to destroy cells, but does not actually "eat" them. The headline-grabbing term most likely refers to the fact that the degenerative condition happens so quickly that it appears the body is being "consumed." (Remember to brush after being eaten!) The infection can be passed from person to person, but even those infected have only a small chance of developing the disease unless they have an impaired immune system, an open wound, or, interestingly, chicken pox.

Might your dentist have the condition and be unaware of it? It's highly possible—especially if he likes "the gas." Though with a surface infection the skin becomes red and hot to the touch, a deeper infection may not present any obvious physical symptoms. In addition, symptoms can develop and become life threatening in just a few hours, as the infection works its way through the bloodstream and begins attacking internal organs. If your gums are bleeding and the dentist's infection isn't visible—but his hands are shaking uncontrollably and the smell of decomposition is in the air—you may want to spit and then swing by the nearest emergency room (bring the dentist with you). Fortunately, *necrotizing fasciitis* can be treated with large doses of antibiotics, though treatment for shock, kidney failure, and breathing problems may also be required. And you probably won't get a new toothbrush.

Or leprosy?

OK, admittedly the chances of your dentist being a leper are slim to none. But, then again, the disease, while rare, has not been eradicated: in 2004 there were about 100,000 new cases—though there were double that many as recently as 1998. Leprosy in nine African, Asian, and South American nations accounts for about 75 percent of the global total. The rest are in your dentist's waiting room. Don't even *think* of picking up that ten-year-old issue of *Highlights*.

Leprosy is a curable disease, but one with a macabre history. The chronic condition has been around at least since ancient China and Egypt, and lepers were typically ostracized and kept in remote leper "colonies" to reduce the spread of the disease. Leprosy is caused by a bacillus (a rod-shaped bacterium) called *Mycobacterium leprae*, and may take five years to incubate. What's more, symptoms may take twenty years to appear—you picked a *really* bad day to go to the dentist—and include severe damage to cells in the skin and nerves, especially in the limbs and eyes. The good news is that transmission is via aerosolized saliva and mucous droplets from the mouth and nose, and infection usually occurs after close and prolonged contact with a leper. If your dentist is wearing a surgical mask, you should be fine. (But if you want to get really freaked out anyway, rent the films *Papillon* and *The Motorcycle Diaries* after your appointment.)

Leprosy is curable when treated early with a combination of three drugs: dapsone, rifampicin, and clofazimine. If you suspect your dentist has leprosy, try to drop *rifampicin* into casual conversation and watch for a reaction.

Quick, before the nitrous oxide kicks in, which condition will it be? Luckily, both are curable with proper treatment. Not so luckily, you are about to drift off into never-never land, and you've got a mouth full of Novocain so you can't say "Stop!" Just remember, if you can't brush after eating, swish and swallow.

WHICH WOULD YOU RATHER DISCOVER IN YOUR SALAD, POISON IVY OR MISTLETOE?

There's nothing quite like a bowl of farm-fresh field greens. Unless, of course, along with the spinach, arugula, and capsicum the salad contains a big helping of toxic plants. No amount of extra dressing is going to disguise this problem, and it's time to choose which leaf is the lesser of two evils, poison ivy or mistletoe. Ingesting poison ivy can be deadly, but if you swallow mistletoe the only kissing you may be doing is your own butt—good-bye.

Poison ivy . . .

It gets a bad rap, and deservedly so: poison ivy is so toxic that 85 percent of the population will develop an allergic reaction to it. It is found nearly everywhere, thrives in disturbed ground (around golf courses, near housing developments), and is extremely fragile—so fragile, in fact, that even a stiff breeze can break stems and cause the toxins to be released. And you don't necessarily have to touch the plant to develop a reaction, either. Almost a third of firefighters who battle forest fires in California, Washington, and Oregon—the three western states where poison ivy is most prevalent—will develop complications from exposure to smoke from the burning plant. Experts highly recommend that you don't go near it. Especially if it's slathered in creamy ranch dressing.

The toxin in poison ivy that causes allergies is called urushiol, a sticky sap (found in all parts of the plant) that can remain on objects (and remain a danger) for years, even *decades*. Though many people require several exposures to develop a reaction, for others a single exposure can lead to painful symptoms. The exposed area will develop contact dermatitis, swelling and becoming red within a day, followed by blisters and severe itching. Symptoms may last for weeks, and have been known to recur because of urushiol trapped in clothes and even under fingernails. Also, different parts of the skin absorb the toxin at different rates, resulting in what appears to be a rash that's spreading. (The oozing blisters do not spread the rash, but scratching them may lead to infection.)

Before taking a forkful of poison ivy, or perhaps setting fire to it with a table candle and taking a long whiff, consider this: if you eat or inhale urushiol, you risk major, possibly life-threatening complications, including dangerous inflammation, swelling, and infection of the lungs, nasal passages, and esophagus. Interestingly, few animals are allergic to poison ivy and many, including birds and deer, eat the berries without problem. Apparently they taste like chicken.

Or mistletoe?

Ahh, the holidays. Chestnuts roasting, carolers caroling, presents under the tree, and severe intestinal trauma caused by ingesting mistletoe berries. There's a very good reason drug stores sell plastic "mistletoe" during Christmastime: mistletoe berries are deadly, and have been known to kill house pets (and even small children) on occasion. Best to kiss close-mouthed if you find yourself under it, and avoid pulling it down, mixing it in with the romaine, and munching on it, too.

The entire mistletoe plant is highly poisonous, though the toxic amines are more concentrated in the berries than the leaves. The history of mistletoe is replete will unusual beliefs and practices. It

 **CHOICE BITS**

* The old saw about poison ivy—"if leaves there be three, let it be"—is accurate, but not comprehensive. Poison ivy can have leaf "clusters" with as many as nine leaves. It also grows in shrub form, not just as a vine.

* The common nickname for mistletoe is the "Kiss of Death."

* European mistletoe, *Viscum album*, is sometimes used in herbal remedies. It is much more toxic than the American variety, but is not sold in the United States.

* If you think mistletoe is dangerous, consider this: a single bite of the "destroying angel," *Amanita virosa*, one of the world's most toxic mushrooms, may cause death.

was burned during Celtic rituals to ward off evil, and was worn around the neck to deter sickness or placed over a baby's crib to prevent theft from fairies. Up until the 1950s, it was even used medicinally, as a treatment for convulsions. It was banned from Christmas ceremonies by the Roman Catholic Church because of its association with paganism. It was never recommended as a vegetable.

Ingesting a large quantity of mistletoe causes numerous, highly serious symptoms, including blurred vision, gastrointestinal distress (vomiting, diarrhea, stomach pain), irregular heartbeat, hallucinations, convulsions, and, if left untreated, death. Because of their small size and weight, pets and small children are at the greatest risk from poisoning, though adults too may be severely injured. Treatment is typically at an emergency room, and includes activated charcoal, along with diagnosis and treatment of related complications.

The good news is that an adult eating just a few berries is not likely to be killed, though severe stomach distress is a virtual certainty. Ninety percent of those treated for mistletoe poisoning within twenty-four hours make a full recovery. The chef, however, is probably looking at a few years of peeling potatoes.

They say some salads (mostly those found at McDonald's) are actually worse for you than the burgers and fries they're replacing. This is almost definitely true if you order the "poison ivy Caesar" or the "McMistletoe salad." But which one to choose? Only one thing's for sure: dessert will be green Jell-O in a hospital bed.

Don't you just love field trips? Permission slips, box lunches, a day away from the classroom—it doesn't get any better. But it can get much, much worse, especially if the field trip is to the Centers for Disease Control, and you're accident prone. And, coincidentally, a careless scientist has left a few deadly pathogens on the counter while she takes a cigarette break. Smashing those vile vials might cause worldwide panic, but that's nothing compared to the choice you've now got to make: black plague or Spanish flu? Oh, and you forged the signature on the permission slip.

Bubonic plague. Pneumonic plague. Septicemic plague. All deadly variations of the dreaded "Black Death" that infamously rampaged across Europe beginning in 1347, in some regions killing up to 50 percent of those infected. How quickly might your fellow classmates (even the ones you actually like) get infected? Very quickly. One reason the plague has killed so many—some estimates are 200 million since the fifth century—is that the bacterium, *Yersinia pestis*, is highly contagious: it can be transmitted in numerous ways, including from the bite of an infected flea, from contact with infected tissue or bodily fluids, and from inhalation. If you knock over that vial, you'd better make a run for the door. Just shove your teacher out of the way.

Bubonic plague, the most common form of the disease, initially infects the lymph nodes, causing a "bubo," a large, inflamed, hemorrhagic node in the armpits and groin. (These lesions range in size, but can get as large as an apple.) After a one-to-six-day incubation period, the infection spreads rapidly throughout the body and attacks internal organs. If left untreated, death results in 40 to 60 percent of cases. During the Middle Ages, rat fleas were the most common carrier (vector) of the disease, and generally poor hygiene and open sewers caused an explosion in the rat population, a "perfect storm" for the plague. Many people seeking to avoid the disease left cities and towns and moved to rural areas, surmising that minimal contact with others might improve their chances of avoiding the plague. This, in turn, left many sick people without caregivers, caused corpses to pile up everywhere, and led to a general breakdown of the social order in Europe. You, on the other hand, would definitely miss a few days of school.

Though the plague still exists today, it is exceedingly rare in the United States (ten to fifteen cases per year) and, internationally, very rare (about 1,500 cases annually). Still, it does turn up in the United States, typically in the desert southwest during warmer months, primarily due to the region's large animal population that can carry the disease. It is treatable with antibiotics. Oddly, the children's nursery rhyme "Ring Around the Rosy" is thought to have been inspired by the plague:

Ring around the rosy (red lesions)
Pocket full of posies (fragrant flowers carried to mask the
    horrible stench of the sick)
Ashes, ashes (death was near or, possibly, the "a-choo" from
    pneumonia)
All fall down (death)

It's probably best not to begin singing this song after you knock over the vial.

Or Spanish flu?

Rat ticks and "bubos" not especially appealing to you? Then consider this: Spanish flu killed more people in a single year than four years of the Black Death in the Middle Ages. Somewhere between twenty and fifty million people perished from the virus, and millions more were extremely sick before recovering. Today, there is still a major possibility that a new "super flu," similar to

Spanish flu, might appear in the wild. If you knock over that flu vial, the plague might seem like a head cold in comparison. And your class definitely *won't* be invited back.

As with the plague, there was a perfect storm for the explosion of the 1918 Spanish influenza pandemic: soldiers around the world were busy mobilizing for World War I, packed together on trains and ships and circling the globe—and spreading the virus, which is transmitted via inhalation or contact with the bodily fluids of those infected. The good news is that most schools were canceled to prevent transmission of the virus. The bad news is that some kids never came back.

The virus, which had (and has) no treatment, causes severe pneumonia and deadly pulmonary complications; most victims died within days of contracting the virus. Quarantine measures, the only effective way to prevent the virus from spreading, were put in place almost immediately, though this led to the deaths of perhaps tens or hundreds of thousands of health care workers. Other strictures to prevent the spread of the virus were unusual: stores could not hold sales, funerals were limited to fifteen minutes, and some towns prevented anyone without a clean health certificate from entering. The effectiveness of such measures, however, is unknown, because Spanish flu could be transmitted from person to person before any visible symptoms developed. So unless you're running a fever in the morning, your parents are probably going to force you to go to school.

Today, influenza continues to be a global health concern, though it typically kills only the very young, the elderly, and those with compromised immune systems. (Spanish flu, on the other hand, killed mostly young and healthy people.) The good news is that, typically, there are effective vaccines for most flu strains. The bad news is that a lethal virus that mutates suddenly, as Spanish flu was thought to, may spread too quickly for a vaccine to be created and distributed. If you did knock over that vial, you, the teacher who planned the field trip to the CDC, and the rest of the world would be in major trouble: no one knows what level of immunity from Spanish flu exists in today's population. And we'd rather not find out. On the other hand, you'd have a great excuse for getting a take-home test.

It's true what they say: no one likes being the one kid who sets off a global pandemic and kills millions. But you don't have a choice. You must pick one or the other, black plague or Spanish flu? Next time, consider suggesting a field trip to the circus.

First dates are so awkward. Flowers or candy? Handshake or cheek kiss? Pick up the check or split it? But what if your decisions are even more difficult, like choosing between a date who has smallpox or one who carries a loaded .38 snub-nose in an ankle holster? Might that rash just be dermatitis? Could she be an air marshal? The decision is yours in this pustule versus pistol matchup.

Smallpox . . .

The bad news is that smallpox was one of history's most feared infectious diseases, a horribly disfiguring virus with no cure. The good news is . . . well, actually there isn't any, except that the virus was thought to have been eliminated thirty years ago. But you do recall your date e-mailing something about "research" and "deadly diseases" and "accident prone." This is definitely the last online match for you.

Smallpox is thought to have appeared in the wild at least as far back as ancient Egypt: the mummified remains of Ramses V displayed deep pockmarks, a hallmark of the disease. It went on to decimate many advanced civilizations, among them the Incas and Aztecs, and in some regions may have had a morbidity rate of 90 percent. "Natural" smallpox (the virus found in the wild) was declared eradicated in 1977, after a colossal World Health Organization vaccination program. But small samples remain in highly guarded research labs around the world—including in the United States.

Smallpox (*Variola major*) is a highly contagious virus transmitted from person to person via mucous, either aerosolized (from sneezing or coughing) or via clothing, sheets, and other contaminated objects. (Animals and insects can't spread it.) The virus has a relatively long incubation period and is difficult to detect because the earliest symptoms include general malaise and fever, both common to many viruses and infections. The contagious phase of the virus begins about a week after infection, signaled by a serious rash. The rash may last ten days, and may be accompanied by severe backache, abdominal pain, and dementia. If your date is clutching her stomach and babbling incomprehensibly even before the oysters are served, you may be in trouble.

Smallpox gets its name from the small, painful lesions (filled with the virus) that appear on the skin of victims after the rash phase. After about a week, the fluid in the lesions turns cloudy (pustular) and the lesions scab over and become round, hard, and deeply embedded in the skin; they typically appear on the face and torso. After several days, the scabs fall off and leave deep scarring. The fatality rate of smallpox in otherwise healthy people is about 30 percent.

It's possible, of course, that your date simply has a serious case of poison ivy. But those scabs—some of which appear to be falling off into the butter dish—are not exactly getting your motor revving. And the guys running into the restaurant dressed in yellow hazmat suits and respirators are not a good sign, either. On the bright side, smallpox is typically only spread via close and prolonged contact, so—unless you plan on waking up next to your date the following morning—a single dinner should not be cause for alarm. Even better, it looks like the waiter is refusing to bring the check to the table.

Or small handgun?

Sure, lots of people probably carry "hideout heat" these days. The Second Amendment says it's our right, and it shall not be infringed. It's like carrying a BlackBerry. Or a cell phone. What's one more handheld gadget in this techno-crazed world of ours? After all, guns don't kill people, only people with mustaches kill people. At least she doesn't have a mustache.

The population of the United States is about 300 million, of whom 143 million are women. There are about 200 million privately owned firearms in this country, and half of all households own a gun. This means that, statistically speaking, every other woman you date is likely to be strapped. To make matters worse, after motor vehicle accidents, firearm homicide was the leading cause of death for men and women aged ten to twenty-four. This means that, statistically, if you didn't get in an accident on your way to the date, you're due to be gunned down.

Of course, many gun owners are not criminals. In fact, according to the National Rifle Association, nobody who uses a gun is a criminal: they are just individuals making preemptive strikes against potential threats that may still be in the planning stages. The handgun strapped to your date's ankle may also be a fashion statement, worn solely to visually balance the ankle monitor secured to her other leg—the one just below her jailhouse "tat." Or she might be in the diamond trade, a courier who carries valuable stones to dealers and needs a "peacemaker" just in case. How else to explain the titanium briefcase handcuffed to her wrist, the one she quietly informs you "is not there"? On the other hand, if she mentions that "either your brains or your signature" are going to be on the dinner check, you may want to climb out the bathroom window.

Which date gets invited home for a nightcap, potential killer or potential killer? Smallpox or small gun? As first dates go, this one doesn't take the cake. But it may take your life, should you choose poorly.

Few things in life are as stressful as an interview for a new job. But you think you're ready: you've researched the company, your résumé is in order, and you've made it there on time. There's just one tiny problem—and it's not the fact that you didn't actually graduate. You've just discovered a critical skin condition, and you've got to deal with it. Fast. But which condition would be worse, a boil on your face or a goiter on your neck? Clearly, it's a much more difficult question than "where do you see yourself in five years?"

Boil . . .

A boil, also called a furuncle, is a fairly common skin infection usually caused by the *Staphylococcus aureus* bacteria (though other bacteria and fungi may also be responsible). The bacteria typically enter the skin at a hair follicle, but then infect the surrounding area, including the subcutaneous tissue. The infection causes a swollen lesion or nodule on the skin, filled with pus. The lesions are typically small, about the size of a pea, but can be as large as a golf ball.

Noticing a boil just before an interview will put you in a bind. A boil may last two weeks, and they typically do not heal until they are drained. Worse, unlike pimples, boils usually do not respond to antibacterial soaps and lotions, or to topical antibiotics. And there's more: the pus inside a boil contains the bacteria, and coming into contact with it may spread the infection; for this reason you should never "pop" or lance a boil yourself, as you would a pimple. Boils will cause tenderness and mild pain, and may be accompanied by fever, fatigue, and general malaise. Occasionally, several follicles next to one another will become infected, the resultant boils will join together, and a large, painful carbuncle will form. In this case, you may need to cancel the interview.

As long as the boil is not draining, you are not in danger of infecting your interviewer (though he or she may be totally grossed out). However, unless your potential job is with a dermatologist, rescheduling may be in order. If the boil is smallish, it may make you self-conscious, as a large pimple would. In this case, consider covering it with a small, round, flesh-colored bandage. Boils may be caused by small splinters, plugged sweat glands, and ingrown hairs. If you catch the boil early, applying a warm compress to increase circulation and bring white blood cells to the area can shorten the duration of the infection. But the interview itself is going to seem like it lasts forever.

Goiters look pretty scary, but in many cases may be relatively benign, and easier to treat than a boil. On the other hand, if a boil can swell to the size of golf ball, then a goiter can be as large as a softball—or larger. A small Band-Aid is not going to do the trick.

The most common type of goiter is a "simple" goiter, which is not the result of disease or another serious medical condition. A simple goiter is typically a visible enlargement of a section of the thyroid gland, which swells as it tries to produce more thyroid hormone to counteract for a deficiency. In a simple goiter, this deficiency is almost always due to a lack of iodine in the diet. Because the body requires iodine to properly produce thyroid hormone, without it the thyroid will enlarge to make up the difference. A minor iodine deficiency may result in a small goiter that is barely noticeable, but a serious shortage will cause major, noticeable swelling. Most people get enough iodine in their diet through iodized salt, which was introduced in the United States in the 1920s to combat thyroid hormone deficiency. If you've cut out all the salt in your diet, it's probably time to start munching pretzels again. Another cause of goiter is excessive consumption of foods that block the body's ability to process iodine. If you've been on a soybean-rutabaga-cabbage-spinach-peach-and-peanuts-only diet, it's time to hit the red meat.

Goiters are usually treated via medication or changes in diet, though a very large goiter with lots of scar tissue may require surgery. Before a job interview, a goiter can be hidden by a large shirt collar, a tasteful scarf (for women), or a cravat (for men).

 **CHOICE BITS**

* Some boils are now being caused by a "superbug" called "community-acquired Methicillin-resistant *Staphylococcus aureus*," or CA-MRSA. This bacterium causes rapid infection and growth of boils.

* Historically, goiters were often seen in people who ate foods grown in iodine-deficient soil. For example, in the English Midlands the condition was so widespread it was known as "Derbyshire Neck."

* Some health experts worry that the trend toward consuming more sea salt and coarse ("Kosher") salt may lead to a resurgence of goiter; these salts are not fortified with iodine.

* Frank Sinatra suffered from goiter.

Another option is a neck brace, though wearing one may result in some awkward questions.

Which condition is preferable just before a job interview, boil or goiter? Minor cases are easy to hide—but we're not talking about those. Severe cases of either will be very hard to disguise, though may make for an interesting ice breaker ("I see you've noticed my boil/goiter. Would you like to know how it makes me eminently qualified for the job?"). Whichever you choose, don't forget to ask about health benefits.

WHICH JOB WOULD BE WORSE, BUILDING THE PYRAMIDS OR BUILDING THE PANAMA CANAL?

Two impressive engineering feats, two massive construc- tions projects, and two very dangerous jobs. But where would you rather toil, in the desert or in the tropics? Among the pharaohs or among the mosquitoes? Either way, Monday morn- ing is going to be hell as you join with tens of thousands of your fellow sweaty laborers to complete one of history's most colos- sal human undertakings. Assuming you're not crushed by fall- ing rock, that is.

Building the pyramids . . .

No, extraterrestrials did not build the pyramids. If they had, you'd be out of a job. The largest pyramid, called the Great Pyramid, was built by a huge (human) workforce for the Pharaoh Khufu around 2530 B.C.E., and was until the twentieth century the largest man-made structure on the planet. Debate continues over the socioeconomic status of those who built the structures— that is, were they slaves or were they paid workers?—but one thing's for certain: it wasn't a job for the weak, lazy, or cowardly. In other words, calling in sick is not an option.

Estimates of the number of workers who constructed the pyramids vary, and depend on assumptions about how long it took to build them. But they range from a few thousand workers toiling over decades to as many as twenty thousand in a shorter timeframe. No matter how many workers it took, the work was difficult. Some of the quarried stone blocks used in construction weighed hundreds of tons, and are thought to have been dragged up ramps by huge gangs of laborers pulling sleds. Working in brutally hot conditions, battling sandstorms, mishaps and injury, and overseers on a schedule, the laborers were not exactly enjoying union benefits. In addition to quarrying and dragging stone blocks and levering or lowering them into position, workers smelted copper for making cutting tools, carted softer stone and soil for ramps, chopped and dragged timber for scaffolding and sleds, and unloaded barges used to transport rock.

Were the laborers slaves who were mercilessly whipped if they didn't work fast enough? It's entirely possible. But current thinking is that they were young men who belonged to tribes or "castes" who would have had little choice but to work on any construction project to which they were assigned. Ancient Egyptian society is thought to have been essentially feudal, and peasants who were born into worker castes probably had little chance of escaping a life of labor. Strapping on the sandals every day and wrapping some fish in papyrus for lunch would have been expected, natural, and unavoidable.

On the other hand, recent archeological evidence suggests that pyramid workers were relatively well fed (as, really, they would need to be), and dined on prime grilled meats, fresh fish caught in the Nile, and fresh bread baked into special loaves more than a foot long. Yum! And, of course, while the weather was undoubtedly hot, at least the sun was shining. If you weren't crushed by a falling stone block or worked to death, at least you could get a tan.

Or building the Panama Canal?

The working conditions on the Panama Canal may have made constructing the pyramids look like building a sandcastle. Between the French and American efforts to open a shipping channel from the Atlantic to the Pacific Ocean, heat, humidity, landslides, and disease led to the deaths of at least thirty thousand laborers, with tens of thousands more sick or injured. In 1904, the average U.S. salary was twenty-two cents an hour. Unskilled laborers working on the canal made a whopping thirty cents. Per day.

By the time American work began on the Panama Canal in 1904, yellow fever—the disease that had wrecked French efforts to build a canal in Panama since 1880—had been linked to the *Stegomyia fasciata* mosquito, which thrived in and around human habitats. A mosquito-eradication program, successfully tested in Cuba several years before, was used in Panama and succeeded in virtually eliminating the disease. Unlike yellow fever, however, malaria was carried by *Anopheles*, a different mosquito variety that was present in virtually infinite numbers in the Panamanian jungle. Worse, unlike yellow fever, malaria did not confer immunity on those who became infected but survived, making the disease harder to eradicate. In 1905, the first full year of work, it is estimated that 100 percent of those laboring on the canal contracted malaria within a month of starting work. How do you feel about those odds?

Workers during the French period faced other dangers. The dump sites for excavated rock and soil were too close to the cuts, leading to huge landslides during Panama's nearly daily rainstorms. The soil, which had a high clay content, was also sticky, and needed to be scraped off shovels and excavating equipment—grueling, backbreaking work. French hospitals in Panama, which had no screens on the windows, were essentially yellow fever and malaria factories, and many injured or ill workers who didn't yet have the diseases refused to visit them for fear of becoming infected.

Canal workers, however, were generally well treated and lived in relative comfort (some in perhaps better comfort than they enjoyed at home). Bakeries and cold storage facilities, complete with ice cream plants, were built on-site. Farms for growing fruit, fresh vegetables, and raising chickens (for eggs) were also added after the first few years. American and European workers could eat in restaurants or mess halls, though West Indian laborers typically had to do their own cooking. Provisions not available on-site were brought in regularly on the Panama Railroad. However, the railroad also did a brisk business in the other

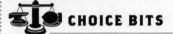

CHOICE BITS

* The Greek historian Herodotus, writing in the fifth century B.C.E., estimated the labor force used to build the pyramids totaled one hundred thousand. However, his claim was made 2,700 years after the pyramids were built and was probably no more than an educated guess.

* The maximum number of workers on the Panama Canal during the American excavation period was about forty thousand, in 1913.

* Though about six thousand workers died under American supervision, most of the fatalities occurred during the earlier French excavation period, from yellow fever and malaria.

direction, shipping the cadavers of dead workers (often stuffed in barrels) to North American medical schools for dissection.

Which construction job would be worse, Egypt or Panama? The Egyptian workers got filet, the canal workers got ice cream. But though they probably had little choice of career, at least the ancient Egyptians only had to answer to the pharaoh. Canal workers had to face rough ridin' Teddy Roosevelt.

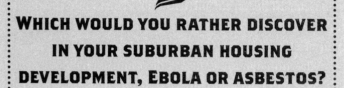

WHICH WOULD YOU RATHER DISCOVER IN YOUR SUBURBAN HOUSING DEVELOPMENT, EBOLA OR ASBESTOS?

Sure, many suburban tract housing developments look the same: two-car garages, two-story foyers, a minivan, and a Volvo. Lawns stay trimmed, kids stay close, and sidewalks are as rare as corner groceries. But what happens when a little excitement hits the exurbs, when bad things happen to good cul de sacs? McMansions are becoming macabre in this matchup of Ebola and asbestos, two very serious problems that put the "ache" in quarter acre.

Ebola . . .

The very word makes the spine tingle. A highly infectious disease with no vaccine and no cure, easily transmitted, and often deadly. Could the pathogen hop the neighbor's fence and make it into your little slice of suburbia? Unfortunately, yes, and a rider mower and a shot of Roundup are not going to take care of this invader.

"Ebola Hemorrhagic Fever" gets its name from the Ebola River, in Zaire (now Congo), where it was first discovered in 1976. Ebola is a zoonotic virus and is carried by animal hosts (possibly bats and/or primates), occasionally mutating and somehow making the jump to humans. Ebola is transmitted through blood, saliva, infected tissue, and mucous, as well as objects that come into contact with them. Unlike most viruses, infection is acute: there is no carrier stage, which means once you are infected, you are immediately symptomatic. Symptoms begin with fever, headache, and joint and muscle aches, and progress rapidly to diarrhea, vomiting, full-body rash and hemorrhaging. There is no real treatment except rest and letting the virus run its course. Mortality rates for Ebola are severe, ranging from 53 to 88 percent, though some people appear to have some immunity. No one knows why.

The virus typically appears "in the wild" only in Africa, and the good news is that Ebola has never appeared in the wild in North America. This means you're unlikely to see the virus in your development, right? Right. Unless you happen to live in suburban Virginia. Or Texas. In 1989 a group of monkeys in a lab in Reston, Virginia, were diagnosed with a form of Ebola later named "Ebola-Reston." The monkeys had been imported from the Philippines. Other monkeys from the same Philippine facility were sent to Texas and were also infected with both Ebola and Simian Hemorrhagic Fever in 1990 and, again, in 1996.

If one of your neighbors happens to be running a primate research facility out of her mud room, calling the authorities is probably a wise move. To lessen the risk of infection, simply continue waving to your neighbors from your car instead of making conversation.

Or asbestos?

You recall the real estate agent mentioning your home's "wonderful fire protection properties" and "great insulation," but you thought she meant smoke detectors and that pink stuff in the attic. Now it turns out the whole development is awash in asbestos and, maybe just as bad, swarming with lawyers.

Asbestos is a general term that describes several naturally occurring, fibrous minerals (similar to fiberglass) that were used for decades in the manufacture of numerous products, among them insulation, fire and sound proofing, flooring tile, roof shingles, chalkboards, packing materials, and many, many more. Asbestos is primarily a hazard when microscopic bundles of its fibers are broken apart, become airborne, and enter the lungs. Once in the lungs, the fibers can cause mesothelioma, a type of cancer, and asbestosis, a disease that scars the lungs when the body produces an acid to try to break down the fibers.

Fortunately, simply noticing (or hearing your neighbors scream) that asbestos is present in the area is no reason to panic. If the material containing the asbestos remains intact and is not in danger of crumbling into dust and becoming airborne, it is typically monitored but not removed. (If there's a fire, then all bets are off.) Also, asbestos exposure is typically a chronic (long-term) health concern, and there have not been conclusive studies on the risks of short-term exposure. If you've just moved in, you're probably fine.

⚖ CHOICE BITS

* Some recent vaccines have shown promise in protecting monkeys—though not humans yet—from Ebola.

* Ebola survivors may experience hair loss.

* There have been more than seven hundred thousand asbestos-related claims filed since litigation began about forty years ago. Companies have paid about $70 billion.

* Asbestos may be found in vermiculite, a mineral used in many garden products, including potting soil.

On the other hand, asbestos remediation is a dangerous, expensive process performed by specially trained technicians, one that will take weeks or months, and will probably make your house uninhabitable while it is occurring. But, naturally, there are hundreds of thousands of asbestos-related lawsuits floating around, and most of them would be happy to have you. Don't worry if you're not sick yet: most of those filing the lawsuits aren't either.

Ebola or asbestos, decisions, decisions. Ebola is rare, asbestos is common. Ebola is a short-term killer, asbestos a long-term one. But to be safe, you might just want to keep a few hazmat suits and portable respirators in the house, perhaps in one of the four empty bedrooms. Thank goodness for all that extra space.

WHICH WOULD BE WORSE, AN APPENDICITIS OR AN AUDIT?

Queasiness. Loss of appetite. Constipation. A sharp discomfort in your stomach, followed by a complicated procedure that could result in serious long-term consequences. Yes, being audited is certainly no fun. But what about appendicitis? Side-splitting pain followed by a visit to the emergency room—if you can make it in time. Not exactly a day at the races, either. Which would be worse, though? It may depend on how creative your accounting is, but either way all your private areas are going to be examined. Under a microscope.

While an IRS audit may take months or years, appendicitis is fortunately a brief affair—often too brief, because if you don't get it treated fast, you could die. (If only the *auditor* got appendicitis. No such luck, however; it's you.) But would you trade a few hours of extreme discomfort for the possibility of a huge fine? Or ten years in the slammer with a cellmate named Bruiser?

The appendix, which has no known function, is a small area of the large intestine where it meets the small intestine. When the inside of the appendix becomes blocked—typically with feces, or from swelling of nearby lymph nodes—swelling results, followed by pain. If the swelling is not treated, the appendix may become gangrenous or, worse, rupture ("burst"). If this happens, hemorrhaging and death may follow.

Like an audit, the early discomfort may seem like a minor annoyance. The pain begins slowly at first, initially around the belly button but then moving to the lower right side (not the left; if it hurts there it's probably gas). Various symptoms that mimic an approaching audit follow, including vomiting, constipation (or diarrhea), and loss of appetite. Talking and even breathing become difficult, bending over excruciating. As the area becomes extremely tender, a sensation called "tenesmus," the feeling that a bowel movement will relieve your pain, may occur. Do not take a laxative, however, and call your doctor, not your accountant: appendicitis is considered a medical emergency.

When the appendix is inflamed, it cannot be treated with antibiotics and is almost always completely removed via a surgical appendectomy. Recovery time may be up to six weeks, but there are no major long-term health consequences of the surgery.

Or audit?

Your chances of being audited by the IRS are actually quite low. In a typical year fewer than 2 percent of all tax returns are picked for audit. The more money you make, however, the greater your chances of getting audited. If you earn more than $100,000 per year, your chances of being audited are about 1.5 percent. But if you earn less than that, your chances drop to less than one percent. Most people who are audited have relatively large itemized deductions and expenses in relation to their incomes, run a cash business, or think they are smart enough to do their own taxes.

Like an illness, an audit may begin innocuously, typically with a thin letter in the mail requesting "more information" about a recent tax return. The letter may cause queasiness even before the envelope is opened, particularly if there is a return address indicating "IRS Audit Division." Indeed, any correspondence at all from the IRS may have you running for the bathroom. The letter itself may note a "discrepancy" and request "additional documentation" to support the claim that your yacht is a home office. The letter may also offer a tantalizing remedy: simply pay what the IRS claims you owe, plus interest and penalties, and the matter will be closed. If you do so, you will be admitting guilt. (Note that being audited in the past, and especially admitting guilt, may increase your chances of being audited

CHOICE BITS

* Most appendicitis patients are under forty.

* Misdiagnosed cases of appendicitis cost the United States $2.4 billion per year in lost wages, hospital charges, and malpractice lawsuits.

* You are much more likely to be audited if you are self-employed.

* The IRS has a "Taxpayer Advocate Service" to protect your rights, especially if you are audited.

again.) There may be a toll-free number to call and request more information about your case. Beware this hotline. It is staffed with persons who have undergone a complicated surgical procedure to remove their hearts and souls. They will be of little help.

If you disagree with the IRS's claims you will need to prove, to their satisfaction, that they are in error. Recently, the "burden of proof" in an audit has shifted from the taxpayer to the IRS, giving you a bit more leeway. However, with bank accounts on the Isle of Man and Vanuatu it may be hard to justify your receipt of food stamps. A complex audit may drag on for months or years, and the outcome will be uncertain. You will be asked to provide receipts, pay stubs, bank statements, and your kindergarten report card. Tax cheats are not simply scofflaws, and cheating on your taxes is a federal offense that can land you in prison—that's how they got Capone, after all. For serious tax evasion, you may be sentenced to five years or more in the big house. If you get a pain in your right side while there, it will probably be a shiv, not your appendix.

Short-term grave illness or long-term headache? Appendix or audit? In short, death or taxes?

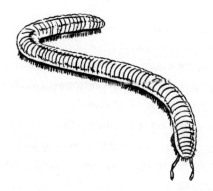

You're armed for battle, with a sword or a shovel. Each sunrise (or sunset) brings a new day (or night) of backbreaking labor, facing injury and death at every turn. You will battle wild animals and risk disease, smell odors that would make a billy goat faint, and risk imprisonment if you fail in your task. But which job would be worse? Granted, skilled gladiators were sometimes treated as heroes, while no one loves a grave robber. But gladiators could fall out of favor and be killed, while grave robbers could be caught and arrested (or shot). The bodies are certain to pile up in this face-off.

Being a gladiator in ancient Rome was a respected, if extremely difficult, pursuit. On the downside, virtually all gladiators were slaves, and fought at the whim of their owners. Because gladiators were highly valuable for their owners, however, they received benefits that were typically not available to the average Roman worker, including expert medical care and plenty of food. A select few gladiators were volunteers (*auctorati*), who probably signed on for a generous bonus and the extra benefits. There were four gladiator training schools in ancient Rome, the largest of which, *Ludus Magnus*, was attached to the Coliseum.

Still, even with the benefits, work as a gladiator was not exactly a day at the baths. The battles were grueling and often (though not always) ended in death. As a special type of gladiator (*bestiarii*), you might face wild animals (*damnatio ad bestias*). Often, the animals—typically lions or tigers, but also bears, on occasion—were starved before a major engagement, to make them more likely to attack. But your most serious challenge is likely to come from other famous and highly skilled gladiators. These combatants were the rock stars of ancient Rome, and graffiti and murals throughout the empire celebrated their deeds. In his rookie season, one freeborn gladiator, Marcus Attilius, defeated Nero's Hilarus, a notable warrior who had more than a dozen victories under his belt. One scribble that was found in the ruins of Pompeii read *Celadus, suspirium puellarum* ("Celadus makes the girls swoon"). Imagine having *your* name up there!

A typical engagement might pit two gladiators with different arms and armor against each other. For example, you might be ordered to battle as a net fighter (*retiarius*) with only minimal armor, your net, and a trident. You would have the advantage of maneuverability, however, and would likely be matched with a heavily armored and lumbering *secutor*. The spectators would applaud and cheer you (or your opponent) as you attacked one another mercilessly until a fatal mistake was made.

The drawback of being a gladiator, of course, is defeat. If you are not killed outright in battle, the sponsor of the match might choose to grant you a reprieve (*missio*). The bad news is that you might just as likely get the "thumb down," and then be summarily executed. The crowd, in a frenzy of bloodlust, would almost certainly cheer for your death, though the sponsor might have to pay your owner a substantial sum for the right to have you killed. But what's a few *denarii* to an emperor? There are plenty more gladiators waiting to take your place.

Or grave robber?

It's a stinking, shameful, low-down, dirty business. You're entering consecrated ground to desecrate the bodies put to rest there, stealing their most treasured possessions, the few things they would have wanted with them when they entered the afterlife. On the other hand, you're the one who knows where all the bodies are buried—not always such a bad thing.

Grave robbing and its even more gruesome sibling, body snatching, have a long and unusual history, going back at least to ancient Egypt. The pharaohs were so terrified of grave robbers that they created highly elaborate burial chambers with secret entrances to deter thieves. These ancient looters would attempt to enter the pyramids and steal the valuables buried with the bodies and thus, the pharaohs believed, prevent them from entering the afterlife. To scare thieves, tombs were often guarded by statues of Anubis, Lord of the Dead, who had the body of a man and the head of a jackal. The ancient Chinese used to inter bodies in suits carved from jade, though virtually all of them were eventually stolen by grave robbers.

It's also said that Michelangelo broke into crypts and stole bodies, which he then used as models for drawings and paintings. Grave robbing became particularly popular in England with the rise of modern medicine and medical courses in anatomy in the early 1800s. Up until this time, by the king's decree, only the bodies of convicted murderers could be dissected—and there were not enough dead murderers to fill medical school demand for cadavers. Two enterprising Irish body snatchers, William Burke and William Hare, went so far as to kill elderly residents of a boarding house and sell their corpses to local doctors. (Though there's no evidence that they actually dug up bodies; they liked them fresh.) In the United States, one famous body snatcher, Dr. Thomas Sewall, was a graduate of Harvard Medical School. Sewall was tried and convicted of multiple counts of grave robbing in Massachusetts in 1819. It didn't hurt his career too much, however, since he later became a professor of anatomy at George Washington University. That Harvard degree *does* open doors.

While grisly, grave robbing can be a lucrative profession. Ancient tombs in South America were often filled with hundreds of pounds of gold coins and artifacts, most of which were looted and either sold on the black market or melted down and recast. Nevertheless, breaking into graveyards is risky business. In addition to the specter of being exposed to the various diseases that may have killed your victims, as a grave robber you'll have to contend with rats and other vermin that feed on corpses—not to mention caretakers with shotguns and various ghosts and ghouls that haunt graveyards and cemeteries in the dead of night. Worse, grave robbing is seriously hard work. It's always the night shift, and you can't operate a backhoe when you're digging up corpses at 4:00 a.m. You and your skeleton crew will be digging with shovels and pickaxes, typically by the dim light of a shrouded lantern on a cold, foggy night. Since all of the tombs in Egypt have already been looted, you'll most likely be digging near a peat bog or some other suitably scary locale.

Gladiator or grave robber, which do you prefer? Gladiators get the fame and the women—if they live. Grave robbers get muddy boots, rotting corpses, and perhaps a few wedding bands. On the other hand, there's always the possibility of stumbling across Jimmy Hoffa. Try to remember where you found the body.

PART THREE
ARCHVILLAINS

In one corner, a fast-moving brute, with hugely muscled legs, powerful jaws, and a taste for flesh. In the other corner, *Tyrannosaurus rex*. True, one's extinct and the other's broke, but in their prime both struck fear into the hearts of their prey. Muhammad Ali could probably take out either one with a right cross, but you're no Ali. You're caught in the alley, and there'll be no rope-a-dope in this fight. Low blows are fine.

T. rex . . .

T. rex was among the last of the dinosaurs to roam the Earth. Despite what movies like *Jurassic Park* might show, humans and dinosaurs never lived at the same time. But what if they had?

Would some unlucky, club-wielding, cave-dwelling early Nean-derthal stand a chance against this monster? Would you? Would a Colt .45 and a sports car make it a fair fight?

Like most modern predators, T. rex would probably shy away from attacking a healthy adult in favor of separating an old, young, weak, or injured individual from the pack. Thus, the best chance of escape would probably be to run into a crowd of people as quickly as possible. Remember, you don't have to be faster than T. rex, you only have to be faster than somebody else. For a large creature, T. rex probably moved at a modest clip, perhaps about twelve miles per hour, though possibly as fast as twenty miles per hour for short bursts. You might be able to sprint to move away, but you would not be able to outrun him for very long. In a car, however, you could easily speed away if you floored it and burned rubber—though it might make for an interesting chase.

The problem, of course, is T. rex's large size and powerful legs, which give the beast tremendous reach. A full-grown male might be forty feet long and could cover a block-long alley with just a few loping lunges. The huge tail helps T. rex keep his balance as he shoots forward into an almost horizontal position and goes in for the kill. His jaws are equipped with sixty-four gigantic, ser-rated, razor-sharp teeth, perfect for inflicting a killing wound and then ripping flesh from bone. Puny and claw-tipped, the beast's tiny arms should not be considered a major threat except perhaps to hold you in place while the descending jaws prepare to crunch you.

T. rex has a keen sense of smell, which he would use to pin-point your position, even if you were in hiding. On the other hand, he might be momentarily confused by strong odors of de-caying meat and rotting garbage, giving you a few seconds to plan an escape. Like a skilled boxer facing a larger opponent, using fancy footwork to outmaneuver T. rex in the alley is probably the best survival strategy. The dinosaur's huge size and bulk, plus the constraints of the walls around it, would make turning around nearly impossible for the carnivore. A good escape plan might include running *toward* the dinosaur and either moving along the wall or running between his legs to get behind him. If the alley was narrow enough, he would be unable to turn around and forced to back out, giving you plenty of time to get away. At that point, it's just a question of running into a crowd of people and letting natural selection do the work for you.

Or Mike Tyson?

Old "Iron Mike" got a bit rusty toward the end of his career in the ring. But in his prime (and probably even washed up) he was a fearsome individual, with a ferocious intensity and brute strength so great that observers claimed many of his opponents took dives just to avoid being injured or killed. (Others would argue most of his early opponents were stiffs.) How might you fare against Mike's famous temper at the end of a dark alley? Don't forget your ear muffs.

In the mid- to late-1980s, in his prime, Tyson was an unstoppable force in the ring, a fighting machine with a lethal combination of intimidation, power, and quickness possibly unrivaled in the history of boxing. A small (under six feet) heavyweight, Tyson fought from the crouch, giving opponents a small target to hit. He punched with rapid combinations more commonly used by lightweights, but he had the power of a larger, heavier fighter. His defensive posture—called "peekaboo" for the way he placed his hands in front of his face—made it that much harder for opponents to land blows to his head. He also had tremendous stamina, going into the late rounds with reserves of power and maneuverability. In 1986, after defeating Trevor Berbick for the WBC heavyweight title, at age twenty and four months Tyson became the youngest heavyweight champion ever. Of course, in his later years he was hobbled by emotional baggage, and fought out of shape and under the influence of antidepressants, leading to a sad decline and his eventual retirement.

Facing down "Kid Dynamite" in an alley—no matter what the year—would not be a pleasant experience. Unlike T. rex, Tyson is not a slow-moving creature and is unlikely to be bested with fancy footwork. In fact, facing a young Tyson would pretty much leave you with zero options, and your best bet would be to take a dive.

Tyson's later fighting style changed—for the worse—to a more open stance, with punches thrown wildly rather than quick jab combinations, leaving his head open to your uppercuts. Because of his relatively short stature, Tyson is vulnerable to opponents with a long reach (like Evander Holyfield). If you happen to have a thirty-six-inch sleeve, you may be able to land a few blows before Tyson moves in close. Finally, low blows and other illegal hits, while effective, may only serve to make Iron Mike angry. And you won't like him when he's angry.

T. rex or Tyson? King of the Lizards or Kid Dynamite? They've tagged it "Don't Dally in the Alley." So whomever you choose, do it quickly. Please. Before Don King shows up.

WHO WOULD YOU RATHER HAVE RUNNING YOUR BLOOD DRIVE, WEREWOLF OR DRACULA?

I t's been said that when you give blood, you give life. But then again it's not supposed to be *your* life. Sure, there are benefits, like the free donuts and orange juice, and the satisfaction that comes from helping others. But what about the downside, like when they can't find your vein? Or when you pass out? Or the fact that due to short staffing the Red Cross has hired Werewolf or Dracula to take your sample? And you've got to choose who will, er, drain your pint.

Werewolf . . .

Your donation is likely to be a hair-raising encounter if a werewolf is seated across from you at the blood drive. Half man and half wolf, legend has it that the werewolf will attack both humans and animals (especially livestock) at any opportunity and—like the wolf—may feed on the flesh of its victims. Werewolves are not known for drinking the blood of their kills, but drawing blood from your arm is certainly likely to whet the creature's appetite. This is particularly true if your blood type is O negative, which of course goes with everything.

"Werewolf" is a contraction of the Saxon word *wer* ("man") and *wolf*. The legend of the werewolf goes back at least to the mythology of ancient Greece, where Lycaon, the first king of Arcadia, was said to be turned into a wolf by Zeus after offering the god a dish of human flesh (*whoops!*). Virtually every country and culture has a werewolf legend, though the details vary with the time and place. In seventeenth century England under James I, before wolves became extinct in Britain, werewolves were said to simply be the victims of witchcraft. In Russia, werewolves were cursed by the devil, while in Norse mythology a group of invincible fighters supposedly dressed in wolf skins. In the 1700s, a huge creature said to be a werewolf terrorized central France, killing livestock. Even as recently as the 1990s, a series of attacks by wolves in Uttar Pradesh spawned a rumor of a man-eating werewolf.

Could donating blood to a werewolf make you a werewolf yourself? If the creature's saliva were to enter your bloodstream (say, while the werewolf bit your neck to extract your donation), you would almost certainly turn into a werewolf on the spot, or at the first full moon. Other things to avoid would be trying on a wolf skin or a belt made of wolf skin, drinking water from the werewolf's footprint, Lon Chaney, and drinking a glass of water from an enchanted stream—make sure that's really orange juice in that cup! Shooting the werewolf with a silver bullet would probably solve your problem, but nobody likes a killing at a blood drive.

Or Dracula?

Naturally, he'd rather draw the blood from your jugular than your arm and he's not big on syringes, but he's offering immortality *and* donuts. And the chance to sleep all day. He's more Bela Lugosi than Brad Pitt, but boy, does he like to party . . . *all night long!*

It's natural to be a little nervous about being stuck by a guy named after Vlad Dracula, also known as "Vlad the Impaler." Dracula ruled Wallachia (now Transylvania, Romania) from 1456 to 1462. His reputation was one of military prowess combined with cruelty and terror, at least when it came to his lifelong enemies, the Turks, and criminals living under his regime. Dracula impaled the bodies of Turkish soldiers and miscreants of all sorts on long stakes, which were then raised high and planted in the ground in the town square, for all to see—at times the stakes numbered in the hundreds. (Though it's worth noting that he was far from the only ruler at the time to use this macabre display.)

The literary figure of the vampire "Count Dracula" was created by the Irish author Bram Stoker in his 1897 novel, based on research of the period. One possible connection between the character Dracula and Vlad Dracula can be explained by stories of incredible cruelty and depravity (not all exaggerated) that were circulated at the time by Saxon merchants unhappy with the ruler's strict trade practices. Rumors and "reports" of ritualistic human sacrifice, bloodletting, and cannibalism probably helped to inspire Stoker as he penned his novel. The real Dracula, like his fictional counterpart, did have several remote and fortified castles high in the mountains of Wallachia, although if he slept in a coffin, turned into a bat, and looked like George Hamilton, there's no record of it.

Dracula at a blood drive might be like *Carrie* at the high-school prom: the novelty would wear off shortly after the mayhem began. But if "da count" managed to keep his fangs in check, he might actually be a pretty effective advocate for blood banks—though leaning more toward withdrawals than deposits. Unlike a werewolf, which might attack you out of anger or boredom, Dracula would probably not suck your blood if he had just fed on a previous donor—at least according to Anne Rice. And even if he did, if nothing else it would be a pleasurable experience, unlike

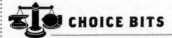 **CHOICE BITS**

* Some experts have postulated that so-called werewolfism was actually caused by erythropoietic porphyria, a congenital condition that includes symptoms such as reddish teeth, hairy hands and face, poorly healing skin, and sensitivity to light.

* Vlad Dracula was so named because his father was nicknamed "Dracul," or "devil"; "Dracula" is a diminutive, meaning "son of devil."

* Count Dracula has been portrayed in the movies by Bela Lugosi, Christopher Lee, Gary Oldman, and Jack Palance, among many other actors.

being ripped to shreds by a werewolf. Dracula would also be relatively easy to deter, using a cross, holy water, a necklace of garlic, or a stake through the heart (though this last method may upset donors who faint at the sight of blood). If all else fails you could move your appointment from 4:00 a.m. to noon.

Jack Nicholson or Tom Cruise? Wolf or bat? Bark or bite? There are no right answers, just bloody difficult questions.

It's *so* difficult to find a good general contractor these days. Just getting one to show up, much less finish what he started, is a battle. Of course, just because your kitchen has been half demolished for six months and all your meals come from the microwave doesn't mean that your job gets priority—besides, there's an emergency at the other job site. But just when you're prepared to put up the drywall yourself, along comes Tony, armed with cell phone and who knows what else. The question is, which Tony do you prefer: Tony "Big T" Soprano or Tony "Scarface" Montana? You might consider hiding the nail gun.

Heavy lifting never scared "T." Unfortunately, most of the lifting was dead weight. Tony notes that your previous G.C. has gone missing—perhaps into witness protection—and now he's offered to help "finish the job." Permits will not be a problem, and he likes to be paid in cash, preferably in a fat envelope. No need to mail the payment, though. He'll send one of his associates around to collect it.

Having the big man take on your renovation project definitely has its advantages. Tony has a large pool of talent to choose from: electricians, plumbers, carpenters, masons, strippers, and more. One possible wrinkle, however, may be that a few of his workers would prefer not to, well, work. If you notice several plus-sized men lounging in lawn chairs in front of the house reading the racing forms, these are the "no work" jobs. Do not confuse these gentlemen with the workers who are on the payroll but don't actually show up. Those are the "no show" jobs.

Like many general contractors, Tony may be too busy to actually oversee the work he's supposed to be supervising. One strategy for getting him to show up is to populate your house with as many scantily clad women as you can find—and the younger the better. Consider renting out a spare bedroom to a young Russian immigrant (a dancer, if possible) to pique his interest. Note, however, that Tony tends to fall hard for unstable women who remind him of his mother. And most of his relationships flame out in spectacular fashion, a particularly undesirable situation which may leave you with a brokenhearted woman and lots of broken furniture.

Like any good contractor, Tony Soprano enjoys receiving

small tokens of your gratitude. Favorites include good cigars (he prefers long "Churchills"); J&B scotch; "gabbagool"; first-class airline tickets; and all-expenses-paid trips to the local casino—plus chips on the house. Offering such gifts may speed up completion of your job. Depending on his mood (which changes by the minute, based on his prescription dosage) he may refuse gifts and prefer that you "owe him a favor" at some unspecified point in the future. Resist the temptation to agree to such an arrangement if possible, lest you find that your home becomes a safe house or a permanent place to stash his "goomar." Finally, do not complain if certain objects of value (Italian marble, fiber-optic cable, your spouse) disappear during the renovations: not all of those lead pipes are for the plumbing.

Or Tony Montana?

Unlike his world-weary, outsized counterpart, the diminutive Montana is likely to bring lots of enthusiasm to your kitchen. Lots and lots of enthusiasm. Just be aware that it's probably chemically induced and all those highs are going to be followed by lots and lots of lows. He too prefers to be paid in cash, and is not a proponent of the income tax.

Never a big fan of manual labor, Tony is likely to play a managerial role in your kitchen project. Like many general contractors, Tony will probably always be on the lookout for a bigger and better project, one that will pay him more money and earn him prestige and power (because you must first get the money, then you get the power). On the bright side, he keeps his word and is not likely to rip you off unless you got it coming. Working with

Tony & Co. requires close attention to every detail, as his interior decorating tastes run toward chintzy gold fixtures, bulky Edwardian furniture, closed-circuit TV cameras, and tigers chained up on their own private islands (but hopefully not your kitchen island).

Should there be any trouble on the job site, Tony is well known to the authorities—and, in fact, may be monitored by them at any time. Like Tony Soprano, Tony Montana is in constant close contact with his attorney. However, in a billing or contractual dispute he's probably more likely to rely on his "little friend" (M-16 assault rifle with grenade launcher) than on his lawyer. Also like his Italian counterpart, Tony can be swayed by the attentions of an attractive woman, particularly one who dresses trashy and dances to bad '80s club music. Still, he is respectful of children (or at least prefers not to assassinate them) and isn't afraid to battle with his "suppliers" over issues of principle. One potential downside to such principled stands, however, is the possibility that a hit squad may invade your brand new kitchen and shoot it to pieces. The world may be Tony's, but it's your house, and you're going to have to clean up the mess.

Two gold-chained, hard-drinking, cigar-chomping contractors, each ready to put in a bid on your under-hung sink and Kohler fixtures. The boss of north Jersey or the peasant from Cuba? Big Tony or little Tony? No matter which man you choose, don't date his sister.

You've tried CTRL-ALT-DEL. You've tried a hard reboot. You've even tried harsh language. But nothing seems to work. It's time to place that dreaded call to the IT department and plead for assistance. Perhaps they'll send Jim, the odorous, lovably unshaven tech dude. Or maybe it will be Why-can't-you-just-use-Linux-and-leave-me-in-peace Matt. Nope, your problem requires a special touch, and it's going to be either the Terminator or *2001: A Space Odyssey*'s HAL 9000. Yes, they're both technically savvy creatures, adept at reformatting your hard drive, exploiting your fears, instilling doubt, and making you nervous. (Then again, so is everyone else in the department.) One of them is on the way up, and he is *really* annoyed with you.

He's big, he's mean, he's dressed in black, and he's definitely *not* from the Geek Squad. They only send him in for the really tough assignments, because he's a master at tracking down and eliminating just about any problem. Or anything that might be a problem at some point in the future. Or, in fact, anything that may or may not be a problem but in any case gets in his way. Windows may finally have met its match.

Cyberdyne Systems Model 101, aka the Terminator, is likely to be a highly focused IT guy, a man of few words but lots of action. Unlike most IT dudes, his "techno utility belt" contains not pager, cell phone, and PDA but Uzi .9 mm, AMT 1911 .45 Long Slide with laser sight, and SPAS-12 automatic shotgun. These weapons may be somewhat effective in battle with your computer, but like all techies he may pay more attention to his gadgets than to your problem. Another possible wrinkle may appear if a second Terminator is called in and put to work on your system. Newer, younger Terminators have a different skill set and tend not to like their older counterparts. A fierce argument may ensue over who, in fact, gets to interface with you and your PC. The older Terminator may be more respectful and protective, while the young "hotshot" is likely to be more intensely focused on getting the job done, no matter what the cost. Also, he will be carrying knives and stabbing weapons, and may be dressed like Erik Estrada from *CHiPs*.

The good news is that any Terminator is highly capable of interfacing with any computer, either by plugging directly into the CPU or via Skynet, the powerful operating system—similar to

Windows—that controls all computer everywhere. Unfortunately, Skynet itself may also be part of your problem, especially if it has become self-aware and is focused on Judgment Day, when it will attempt to destroy all humans on the planet and take over. Should this be the case, the Terminator may be required to make a very long tech support call to Cyberdyne Systems, the company—similar to Microsoft—that created Skynet before it got too big and went out of control. This call may be routed to Bangalore. The Terminator could ultimately be forced to travel back in time to 1984, to assassinate the person most directly responsible for inventing the software that took over all our lives. If you get in his way you, too, will be scheduled for termination. Best not to interfere, since he'll be back.

Or HAL 9000?

Don't be lulled by his soothing voice, seeming lack of emotion, and antiseptic, machinelike exterior. HAL is actually a deeply disturbed techie who thinks he knows what's best for your computer *and* for you. Should you attempt to interfere with his actions, he will attempt to disable your PC and then try to kill you. At least he doesn't ride a Harley.

As the "brains" behind all of your office's computer systems, HAL isn't likely to be caught unaware when a PC has a meltdown. In fact, like a firefighter turned arsonist who wants to be called in to save the day, HAL may actually be responsible for all of your system's odd behavior. Should you suspect this is the case, do not voice your suspicions to workmates or to any other IT personnel: HAL is fully capable of reading lips. Do not send an e-mail, either.

An übertechie, HAL, should he choose to do so, can readily inform you of the problems plaguing your PC. But though HAL has been programmed for "the accurate processing of information without distortion or concealment," if he determines there to be a contradiction between his hardwiring and a specific command, he will simply kill you to eliminate the potential conflict. If angered or trapped, HAL may fall into the role of vengeful IT dude, sowing confusion and terror by infecting the network with a virus, corrupting critical files, spoofing e-mail addresses and sending threats to coworkers, and signing you up for massive amount of spam. He may also delete all your porn.

Terminator or HAL? Which is the lesser of the two evils? In a sense, it doesn't really matter. Whatever your choice, you're never going to call the IT department for help again. Perhaps that was their plan all along.

They both look terrific in black, though Don Vito favors a tux while Vader prefers a cape. They both have sons who are repulsed and yet strangely attracted to their way of doing business. And they both have daughters who are troublemakers. In essence, they are family men, but with major family problems. But there's room at the dinner table for one more place setting, and the adoption papers are all in order. Which villain would make the better (or worse) father? As the old saying goes, you can't pick your parents. But if you *could*, imagine making this choice! Don't fret, though. In five years the family will be completely legitimate.

Give the Dark Lord his due: Vader's powers of persuasion are pretty spectacular. His whole "join me and we'll rule the galaxy as father and son" schtick has a *real* nice ring to it. Forget Ewoks and Aunt Beru—on the Dark Side, it's all there for the taking! Death Stars! Slave droids! Intergalactic mayhem! And yet . . . and yet . . . something doesn't feel quite right. Can Vader really be trusted? After all, he did freeze Solo in carbonite—and he tried to get you, too. Not exactly a welcome-to-the-family hug.

As a dad, Vader would likely be a strict disciplinarian, firm and not always fair. (Best not to fail him a second time.) His megalomaniacal obsession with wiping out the Rebel Alliance, blowing up planets, and imprisoning or killing all your friends points to serious control problems. And his desire to see your sister killed may serve as a warning of major intimacy issues. Darth also has little patience for incompetence, and tends to strangle first and ask questions later. He may also view your past relationship with Obi-Wan as a threat to his new role as "Dad," especially since your Jedi master is now more powerful than Vader could possibly imagine. It's probably best to keep your conversations with Kenobi private, at least until you get settled in.

On the plus side, on good days the two of you could enjoy some quality recreation time together, fencing with light sabers, straightening up your Imperial Star Destroyer using only mind control techniques, and having TIE fighter races. Loser buys lunch! Plus, let's face it, you've got anger management issues, too. The Dark Side has always exerted a strong pull on you. Who doesn't like being the bad boy now and then? It's just so hard to get rid of the hate. But only the good die young, right?

Or Don Corleone?

Should Don Vito find out that he's competing with Vader for your affections, you can bet he will put out a contract to have Darth taken out by someone "close," perhaps Boba Fett. Or he could try intimidation. Might Darth Vader possibly wake up one morning with the severed head of a tonton in his bed?

They may have scared a movie producer like Woltz, but the Godfather's intimidation tactics are unlikely to work in this situation. Instead, the don will probably welcome you into his large home, introduce you to your new siblings—watch that Sonny, he flies off the handle—and give you a position in the family business. But will it be running Genco Olive Oil, or running a casino in Vegas? It could be the latter. Word on the street is that, within a week, you're going to move Klingman out.

Entering the Corleone clan (and, by the way, it's pronounced "Core-lee-own" not "Core-lee-own-ee") has its advantages over throwing your lot in with Vader. Forget ruling the galaxy, you'll be running New York! Admittedly, you'll be in a power-sharing situation with the other families, but you will have the gambling, the prostitution, and all the judges and politicians in New York in your back pocket. (At any rate, your pop will have them.) Those, of course, are the best things to have. You'll also enjoy playing with kittens, granting favors, shopping for produce, and perhaps visiting Sicily.

Like Vader, Don Corleone has strong feelings about what he

⚖️ CHOICE BITS

* The horse head Don Vito orders placed in Woltz's bed was real; it was acquired from a dog-food factory just before filming.

* Brando refused to memorize most of his lines and as a result had to read from cue cards.

* The cat in Brando's lap was a stray he found on the Paramount lot that was written into the film. The cat's contented purring on the don's lap was so loud much of the star's dialogue had to be "looped."

* The voice of Darth Vader was originally provided by David Prowse, the six-foot, seven-inch British actor who played him in the first several movies; James Earl Jones's voice was added later.

* Darth Vader is ranked number three on the American Film Institute's list of fifty top villains of all time. Michael Corleone is number eleven. Hannibal Lecter is number one.

wants for his sons' futures, and he doesn't appreciate when his orders are not followed. You'll be entering an extremely complicated family dynamic, one that already has established roles for the wise son, the favorite son, the wild son, and the "smart" son who craves respect. Further, your new sister has major trouble picking decent men, and you may be called upon to, say, slam a trash can on some stiff's head if he gets out of line. Your new dad is also very secretive, and disdains talking business outside the family—or at the dinner table, for that matter.

The good news is that, should you choose Don Vito as your new dad, you may eventually become a senator or a governor, should he wish it. The bad news is there may not be enough time, and you'll end up having to kill your brother, your sister's husband, a police captain, and various family acquaintances.

Will it be Daddy Darth, or Daddy Don? If it's power you crave, this could be your dream decision. Of course, they're both living on borrowed time. And, truth be told, neither one is likely to win father of the year.

WHO WOULD YOU RATHER HAVE AS A HIGH-SCHOOL CHEMISTRY TEACHER, ALIEN OR PREDATOR?

High-school science class is dangerous enough as it is: over-worked teachers, unruly teenagers, and toxic chemicals are a combustible mixture. Throw in a clumsy kid or two, a Bunsen burner, and a vial of hydrochloric acid and you've got the makings of an experiment in evacuation on your hands. But what happens when the most deadly part of the whole period is up at the head of the class, searching for a few volunteers? Nails across the blackboard are going to be the least of your worries in this monstrous matchup of teacher Alien versus Mr. Predator. Please put on your safety goggles.

Word in the lunchroom is that teacher Alien has *quite* the temper. And his hygiene—what with all the drooling—is not the best, either. Then again, chemistry teachers are known for their little eccentricities. Could Alien finally be the motivator the school board has been looking for?

Alien is likely to keep his lab on the warmer side, which could lead to lots of drowsy students. Falling asleep, however, is hardly a recipe for success in his classroom: rumors abound that some kids have been sent to "detention" and never heard from again. A strict disciplinarian, teacher Alien will not tolerate distractions of any kind. Initial disruptions are likely to be met with a whack from the tail, while subsequent infractions could lead to the teacher lurking just over your shoulder, slobbering, and breathing into your ear. Should Alien decide that corporal punishment is appropriate, you may be able to defend yourself with a pulse rifle or a flamethrower. Weapons in the classroom, of course, will be dealt with harshly.

Most of the experiments in teacher Alien's laboratory are almost certainly going to involve acid. You may be issued a helmet and body armor to protect you during labs, but be aware that the acid is extraordinarily caustic and will burn through pretty much anything. Alien has a solid grasp of the human anatomy, and other experiments may be geared more toward biology and genealogy, particularly propagation of the Alien's own species. To this end, you may notice long rows of egglike sacs that peel open as the petals of a flower to reveal spiderlike creatures seeking to attach themselves to your face. From this point, it's just a short trip to the school's basement, where the building's heat exchanger will keep you warm during, er, sleepovers.

Alien may be out of the classroom for long stretches of the school year as he jockeys for power with administrators and other teachers. In these cases, his classes are likely to be taught by a substitute teacher, also named Alien. If the substitute turns out to be his mother, best to be absent that day.

Or Predator?

Mr. Predator is a highly intelligent, highly evolved life-form, one that perhaps surpasses even teacher Alien in his disdain for troublemakers in the classroom. His reliance on advanced technology (lasers, heat-based vision), however, could put him at a relative disadvantage in an under-resourced school district.

Initially, students could be put off by Predator's unusual appearance: very long nails (almost claws, really), dreadlocks, lizardlike skin tone, and belt of skulls. However, once he activates his camouflage, you'll barely even notice him. (This may be particularly disconcerting during tests and quizzes.) Unlike teacher Alien—who universally dislikes pretty much everyone—Mr. Predator tends to single out the bullies, troublemakers, and the well-armed for special consideration. And like all good teachers, Predator enjoys a challenge and is not one to back down from a confrontation: Gang members may be at particular risk in his chem lab. But if you play by the rules, follow his lesson plans, and don't have a particularly large cranium, you should be fine.

Science is always hands-on in Mr. Predator's classroom. Experiments may involve really fun and creative uses of gunpowder,

⚖ CHOICE BITS

* Tom Skerritt, who played the role of Dallas in *Alien*, was originally cast as Warrant Officer Ripley, the role that made Sigourney Weaver a star.

* Jean-Claude Van Damme was the original Predator but quit the movie after learning he would basically be a special effect.

* Some observers claim the plot of *Predator* closely follows the epic *Beowulf*.

the construction of plasma cannons and lasers, and designing wrist-mounted self-destruct devices capable of vaporizing the classroom, the school, and the school district. (Should this last device be activated accidentally, just duck behind a desk and you'll be safe.) Predator should have a small medical kit handy in case of emergency. A note on his appearance: Mr. Predator has a large jaw and prominent incisors (or "mandibles") that give his face a crablike appearance. A bit self-conscious, he tends to wear a large helmet in public to hide these features. Students who call him "ugly" tend to regret it.

Chemistry has rarely been as exciting (or dangerous!) as it will be with Alien or Predator mixing things up. But which creature would really make the subject come alive? Forget dipping roses in liquid nitrogen and shattering them with a hammer. Should you choose poorly, this year they'll be sweeping up *your* pieces.

Sleepaway camp is traumatic enough as it is, what with the separation, the bullying, and the inedible food. But this year, the calls home aren't going to be due to homesickness—and they may be monitored, for your protection. Those won't be crocodile tears, either, because there's a new face in your bunk. If you thought swimming in the lake was sheer terror, meet your newest counselor, Dick or Osama.

Dick Cheney . . .

True, he's the only counselor with a serous heart condition. And, granted, he's a bit out of shape—even for tetherball. But Dick's made it very clear that his number one goal is the safety and security of all campers at all times. Because, as he says, your rivals in Camp Jihad across the lake "are preparing to attack" Camp Patriot at any moment. Capture the flag is for amateurs. This year, it's all-out war.

Counselor Cheney is certain to wield his power behind the scenes, convincing other counselors—especially gullible, green CITs—to do his bidding. In fact, there have been pretty convincing rumors that the unintelligent, inexperienced camp director really answers to "Camp Cheney," a highly secretive "shadow camp" that actually makes all the decisions and runs the larger camp. Cheney also has a cadre of underlings (known as JCs or "Junior Cheneys") who leak damaging information about unruly campers to the camp newsletter. Counselor Cheney has a vindictive streak, and may punish wayward campers by spreading rumors of bedwetting and other "unpatriotic" actions. Campers who refuse to go along with his activity schedule may be tagged as "traitors" or not sufficiently supportive of the camp and its policies. An avid hunter, Cheney will most likely be put in charge of the rifle range. Note, however, that his enthusiasm may get the better of his aim.

Cheney will probably institute new disciplinary measures in your cabin to keep difficult bunkmates segregated from the general cabin population. A purpose-built "detention cabin" will house "seditious" campers suspected of seeking to sneak dates into cabins, clogging the toilets, carving their names into the rafters, and bringing down the camp administration. These campers may be blindfolded, fed a diet of nothing but bug juice and Scooter Pies, and subjected to "rendition" to mommy and daddy. Their camp fees will not be refunded, either. Counselor Cheney may also seek a new fee policy whereby the costs for more affluent campers are lowered while those for more needy campers are raised. This policy will, according to Cheney, spur wealthy campers to invest in the camp and make improvements that will help all campers equally.

Or Osama Bin Laden?

Let's be honest: Bin Laden knows *a lot* more about working in camps than Dick Cheney. He's also an experienced hiker and horseman who has no trouble living off the land and retreating into the wilderness when necessary (though he'd prefer access to a satellite phone). Could your summer at Camp Jihad be the best one yet?

Osama has been very proactive in courting you and your parents, going as far as sending you a "meet the counselors" videotape espousing his "camp ideology" and voicing his contempt for your archrivals over at Camp Patriot. At Camp Jihad, you'll learn how to fire an assault rifle, burn a flag, and drive a fully loaded car or truck at 90 miles per hour while weaving left and right. How fun! Of course, counselor Bin Laden himself may not be present during all activities, particularly when Camp Patriot's spy satellites are passing overhead. But his retinue of followers, admirers, and hangers-on are happy to carry out his orders—or even make decisions on their own.

At Camp Jihad, the organizational structure is slightly different than at your average Catskills summer camp. Campers are divided not by bunk but by "cell." In fact, you may not even get to live with the other campers in your cell: you will meet up with them at activities or just before your mission begins. Sleeping quarters will be cots in military-style tents (or caves, if available), and campers will be expected to do their own laundry—no need for nametags!—and clean their own rifles. Friday will not be pizza day.

Counselor Bin Laden will plan general camp strategy, handle the finances, and oversee multiple cells. His second-in-command, Ayman "Skip" Zawihiri, will handle day-to-day activities such as indoctrination, arts and crafts, tunneling, swimming, and communicating in code. Bin Laden's overall goal for the camp, of course, is the destruction of the "imperialists across the lake," Camp Patriot. To this end, you and your fellow campers may be called upon to sneak into the camp, pose as "patriots," learn their ways, and then attempt to destroy the camp through subversive activities. Note, however, that unlike Camp Jihad, Camp Patriot welcomes girls and the dining hall serves soda with caffeine. Do not be swayed by their decadence.

Eight weeks can seem like forever, or it can be over before you know it. It all depends on how much fun you're having. But nothing can ruin a summer at camp like a bad counselor. So remember, you've got to live with this guy every day. Camp Patriot or Camp Jihad? Cheney or Bin Laden? Word around the lake is they both snore.

The guests are all making themselves comfortable in the living room, the bar is open, and the iPod is set on shuffle. It's going to be a wonderful evening of stimulating conversation, quick-witted banter, and . . . mayhem. The catering team has just arrived, they are pouring out of the van, and they don't match the photos on the website. What's more, they are heavily armed, and not just with paring knives. But which group of ne'er-do-wells would be worse, Neanderthals or ninjas? At least the ninjas are wearing black . . .

When they said "club fare," apparently they meant it literally. But come to think of it, the guy on the phone wasn't exactly a conversationalist; in fact, he mostly just grunted. Now you've got a pack of hirsute cavemen in the kitchen, and none of them are wearing hair nets.

The good news is that Neanderthal men were carnivores but probably not cannibals (unless it was an emergency). The bad news is that your cat may be in serious danger. Neanderthals—named after the Neander Valley, near Düsseldorf, Germany, where remains were discovered in the nineteenth century—were prolific hunters. Because they lived during the most recent ice age (the Pleistocene period), Neanderthals probably subsisted on a diet primarily of meat, which accounts for their huge, powerful jaws and preference for pigs in blankets and Spam. One potential problem may be their befuddlement at your vast array of knives and chopping tools. Neanderthal man tenderized his kills either by chewing them thoroughly or by pounding them flat with a wooden club. (On the other hand, chemical meat tenderizers won't be necessary.) Another roadblock may be his poor (or nonexistent) language skills. It's probably safest to direct Neanderthal man to smile warmly at your guests and nod politely when they take food off serving trays. Dressing the servers as mimes may not be a bad idea—though loincloths may give your soiree a hip, Flintstones feel.

As a caterer, Neanderthal man is likely to skip the crudités and focus on spit-roasted meats such as saber-toothed (or cave) tiger, mastodon (if in season), and dodo (market price). Sushi is out. Consider disabling your smoke detectors unless you want the open-pit fire in the kitchen to disrupt the party. One thing to watch out for is dissension in the kitchen, something common among caterers and cavemen when things get a little hectic. Profanity isn't likely to be a major issue, but your guests may be put off by the screaming, chest thumping, club fights, and murderous rage. And should Neanderthal caterer take a shine to one of your attractive female guests, well, suffice it to say that having her dragged into the kitchen by her hair is not likely to land you positive coverage in the society pages. When all else fails, put the nature channel on the kitchen TV and keep *neanderthalensis* away from the booze.

Or ninjas?

They come in like the breeze—so quietly, in fact, that you may not even notice their arrival. Well trained in the black arts of high-heat wok cooking and stir-fry, skilled with cutlery, and ready to skewer just about anything, ninjas will get the job done with minimal fuss.

The problem, of course, is that they tend not to stick around to clean up the mess. Another possible hurdle is that, as an unaffiliated band of caterers wandering the countryside in search of paying jobs, the ninja may not be especially loyal, always seeking a more lucrative engagement and possibly leaving you in the lurch come party time. The term *ninja* derives from the Chinese pronunciation of two kanji characters, *nin* (meaning concealment)

CHOICE BITS

* Recent discoveries indicate that Neanderthal's physiology was similar enough to *Homo sapiens* to allow for some form of speech, if not true language.

* Neanderthals used stone tools and weapons, as well as those made from wood, bone, and antlers.

* Ninjas often did not dress in black but rather wore the garb of their enemies to more effectively blend in, allowing them to get close enough to kill.

and *sha* (person). It may be helpful to keep this information in mind when something in the oven is burning and you're running around the house looking for your chef/ninja. Check walls and ceilings to make certain the catering staff isn't up to their old ninja antics. Cookies and other small, aerodynamic food items may be served as *shuriken* (throwing stars), flung at unsuspecting guests when their backs are turned.

A skilled ninja caterer should be able to slice the top off a bottle of champagne with his sword in a flash. Unfortunately, he's equally skilled at lopping off heads, and rude guests may be marked for assassination—or at least ignored when the hors d'oeuvres come around. The ninja catering team is not likely to make small talk with your guests, a positive if you feel wait staff should be seen and not heard. Exercise extreme caution when inviting samurai to your event: in this case, the catering staff must stay in the kitchen and keep their swords in their scabbards at all times. All food items should be checked for poison before serving.

Who's going to stuff the mushrooms caps and slice the prime rib, Neanderthal man or ninja guy? Who will be the new Iron Chef? It's strength versus stealth, stone age versus swordsman in this kitchen cook-off. You do have a double oven, right?

PART FOUR

KILLER CREATURES

WHICH WOULD YOU RATHER DISCOVER IN YOUR BACKYARD, A WEST NILE MOSQUITO OR A WEST AFRICAN DICTATOR?

A h, summer. Warm breezes, cool drinks, the scent of freshly cut grass, and smoke from the barbecue. You've got the afternoon off, a roast beef sandwich, and a trashy novel. Nothing's going to ruin *this* day. Except the viral mosquito landing on your face or the psychotic African dictator lounging on your patio— *and* he's drinking your beer! Two bloodthirsty killers, one very tough decision.

West Nile mosquito . . .

You were planning on a slight buzz, but this isn't exactly what you had in mind. In addition to being an annoying irritant, a mosquito carrying West Nile virus (WNV) is a potentially deadly intruder.

The good news is that most people (four out of five, on average) show no symptoms after being infected with WNV. The bad news is that you could be the one who does. Sure, a quick slap will take care of the problem. But what if you fall asleep? Then it's skeeter feeding time, and your blood is the main course.

WNV has been around at least since the late 1930s, though the virus and its effects were not well understood until the 1950s, when an outbreak in Israel resulted in cases of severe meningitis and encephalitis (inflammation of the spinal cord and brain, respectively). The virus spread through Africa and then into Europe, reaching the United States in 1999, with the first documented cases of WNV-related encephalitis in humans and horses. Since then, the virus has spread rapidly, via birds and mosquitoes, and has been discovered in every state except Alaska and Hawaii. You live in one of the lower forty-eight.

It takes just seconds for an infected mosquito feeding on a human to transmit the virus. Once infected, the itching will be the least of your problems. WNV victims will experience fever, headaches, muscle aches, nausea, and vomiting. Typically these symptoms will last a few days, but in some people full recovery could take weeks. For an unlucky few—perhaps one in a hundred and fifty—the virus will progress to tremors, convulsions, coma, vision loss, paralysis, and permanent disability—and even death, in rare instances. Worse, there is no specific vaccine or treatment for the virus: in serious cases, palliative care at a hospital is usually the only course of action.

Mosquitoes are easier to avoid than pesky dictators. Many species are most active at dawn and dusk, and all of them require standing water to breed. Unlike dictators, they won't hang out or try to breed in your pool, due to the chlorine and other chemicals. Mosquitoes are crafty, however, and can sense body heat, breathing, and movement from at least a hundred feet away. They are also attracted to bacteria produced by human feet—the same bacterium found in Limburger cheese, incidentally, which helps explain the smell—which is why most bites occur there. Short of staying indoors or under mosquito netting, the best way to avoid WNV is to wear long sleeves and pants, apply bug repellent, or move to Alaska or Hawaii. But then you'll have to worry about bears and volcanoes.

Or West African dictator?

Which West African dictator would you rather have sunning himself on your back porch? That's a bad vs. worse showdown in its own right. For the sake of argument, we'll choose Charles Taylor, former president of Liberia, preacher, warlord, escaped convict, diamond smuggler, gun runner, snazzy dresser, and current war criminal to be tried in The Hague. Sure, there are other dictators from the region, but few as flamboyant. Or as certifiable.

Charles "Ghankay" Taylor—he added the middle African name late in life, to appeal to indigenous voters—was born in Liberia but educated in the United States. Before showing up in your yard, he served in the government of Samuel Doe, who took over Liberia in a 1980 coup. After being accused of embezzlement, Taylor fled to the United States where he was jailed in Massachusetts, awaiting extradition. Amazingly, he escaped, though there are varying explanations of how he accomplished this feat. He and several other inmates filed down the bars in a jail window, then climbed down bed sheets to safety. However, some speculate that the CIA aided his flight, hoping he would return to Liberia and overthrow the Doe regime (which he later did). Regardless, he's not likely to be content with hanging out on your deck furniture for very long, and you should expect a knock on the screen door at any time.

On the bright side, Taylor enjoys table tennis and lawn tennis, and is said to be a highly skilled player. He may even challenge you to a game in your yard. Let him win. Taylor likes to be called "Pappy," which reminds him of happier times when he commanded a vicious army of drug-addicted child soldiers who often dressed in costumes and blond wigs. (Best to keep your kids in the house.)

After being "elected" Liberia's president in 1997—famously, his election slogan was "He killed my Ma, he killed my Pa, but I will vote for him"—Taylor ruled the country through a period of

 **CHOICE BITS**

* Only female mosquitoes feed on blood, which provides the proteins they need to lay their eggs.

* The chemical NN-diethyl-meta-toluamide (marketed commercially as DEET) confuses the mosquito's chemical receptors and is one of the only proven means of preventing mosquitoes from biting.

* Charles Taylor has a degree in economics from Bentley College.

* Taylor is annoyed by mosquitoes.

turmoil and bloody battles with rebels until his forced resignation in 2003. Taylor may try to bribe his way into exile in your home with a fistful of diamonds (Liberia is rich in gemstones) or a free set of snow tires (Harbel, Liberia, is home to the Firestone rubber plantation, the largest in the world). He may also try to appeal to your sense of morality by calling on his friend Pat Robertson, with whom he has had extensive business dealings.

Hopefully, Taylor won't invite any of his dictator buddies—among them Libya's Muammar Qaddafi and Sierra Leone's Foday Sankoh—over for beer and burgers. Still, he can be charming and you may enjoy his company for a while. At least until he pits your neighbors against you, throws you out, and takes over.

Two dangerous visitors, out for blood. You may end up in the hospital—or worse. Or you could just shut the door, crank up the AC, and hope they take a shine to your neighbor.

WHICH WOULD BE WORSE TO FIND IN YOUR SLIPPER, A BLACK WIDOW OR A GIANT CENTIPEDE?

A comfortable old pair of slippers. You start to feel relaxed as soon as you ease them on. Shuffling around the house, perhaps in your robe, you hold a steaming mug of freshly brewed coffee. Life is good. But wait. What's that funny feeling? Forget the odor and the sweat, these old slippers have a *truly* nasty surprise waiting for your calloused dogs. That nibbling at your toes is either a black widow spider or a South American giant centipede. Which is worse, eight legs or forty-two?

Black widow . . .

The name alone is enough to set your hair on end. Compact, really scary looking, very dangerous, and common to boot—at least in many parts of the country. (Note that a northern black widow, a similar species, may be dark brown, not just black.) Probably not the arachnid you want to play footsie with.

The black widow (*Latrodectus mactans*) is arguably the most poisonous spider in North America. It is a carnivorous predator, typically feasting on roaches, flies, beetles, and anything else it can catch and poison. It will attack if poked, prodded, or accidentally disturbed by a human—or a human foot. The good news is that only female black widow spiders are dangerous. The bad news is that you're much more likely to encounter a female, since males may be killed and eaten soon after they mate. (Juveniles are harmless.)

The bite of a female widow may go unnoticed, especially since there is typically not much swelling. In some people, however, the bite can be incredibly painful and can cause severe health complications; it can even be deadly, especially to children and the elderly or infirm. As it bites, the spider injects a strong neurotoxin. The poison quickly travels through the bloodstream and acts on the central nervous system, often causing intense pain. Pain tends to radiate out from the injection site and settle in the lower back and abdomen, and symptoms like labored breathing, tremors, and nausea are common. Unlike the giant centipede, black widows are not foragers. They spend most of their time hanging in the web, upside down (abdomen up), making their reddish "hourglass" marking easily visible. Discovering a black widow in your slipper is unlikely, though not impossible. If you've left your slippers out by the woodpile for a few days, best to shake them out before putting them on.

Or giant centipede?

A centipede is never going to win any beauty contests, even when paired with a black widow. Mostly, however, they're ugly and harmless. But the one that's made it into your slipper is the Godzilla of centipedes, and your wriggling toes look pretty much like lunch.

The giant centipede (*Scolopendra subspinipes*), while large in comparison to other centipedes, typically only reaches about six inches in length—though some tropical specimens may be longer than your forearm. The giant centipede is nothing like the tiny creatures you see darting around your house. It's the most dangerous and toxic of all centipedes. The creature has two large, poisonous fangs used to inject a paralyzing venom. The largest specimens have been known to attack and devour birds, rodents, and small invertebrates like geckos, as well as other centipedes. (No word on their preference for smelly feet.) While they do not have the hundred feet their name implies, they do have lots, one pair of feet/legs per body segment—which, incidentally, means they are not insects, which have six legs. They move extremely quickly and are known to be aggressive.

The bite of the giant centipede is extremely painful, and its toxin can be deadly to house pets and small children. A bite to a healthy adult is likely to be very uncomfortable but not deadly. On the downside, the centipede is a wandering predator. It is extremely active and often enters buildings and small indoor spaces in search of prey. Human encounters are not unusual, and if surprised a giant centipede will bite in an instant.

 **CHOICE BITS**

* The silk from a black widow is stronger than an equal-sized filament of steel.

* Black widows have poor eyesight.

* After injecting its venom, the black widow sucks out the liquefied insides of its prey.

* The fast-moving centipedes you see in your house are, appropriately enough, "house centipedes," and are generally harmless to humans. The bad news: they feed on roaches and other household insects, so if you see lots of them, you may be infested.

Eight-legged freaks or forty-two-legged freaks? Small and stealthy or big and fast? Black widow or giant centipede? It's your foot, so it's your choice. Next time, consider shoe trees.

──

**WHICH WOULD YOU RATHER NOTICE
SWIMMING BELOW YOUR INNER TUBE,
A BARRACUDA OR A PORTUGUESE
MAN-OF-WAR?**

──

Steven Spielberg hasn't made a horror movie about barracuda or jellyfish yet—though, granted, those killer alien ships in *War of the Worlds* looked conspicuously like gigantic jellyfish—but that doesn't mean they aren't dangerous. Sure, sharks get all the glamour and their own week on the Discovery channel, but there are many other fearsome fish in the sea. A barracuda or a man-of-war may not kill you, but they can certainly ruin your day at the beach. Which one would you rather face—or have facing your behind?

─────────────── **Barracuda . . .** ───────────────

It's sometimes called the "tiger of the sea." (Not to be confused with "chicken of the sea." That's tuna.) A great barracuda can be over six feet long and weigh more than one hundred pounds. And its teeth are like miniature daggers, perfect for ripping apart flesh. It's a long, lean, mean killing machine. Oh, and it's pretty ugly, too.

The barracuda is at least fifty million years old, and its durability is testament to its adaptability: it will swim alone or in schools, hunt among reefs and shoals or in the open sea, and eat pretty much anything it can catch. Unlike a shark, a barracuda will typically not attack a human if unprovoked. However, the fish is aggressive and will readily bite if trapped or harassed, and may attack if confused by conditions of poor visibility. Barracuda are also extremely common, and live in tropical or subtropical waters around the world. In particular, barracuda can be found in the Atlantic from Massachusetts to Brazil, as well as in the Gulf of Mexico and the Caribbean.

Would a hungry barracuda chase you in your inner tube? It's certainly not likely to be afraid of you, since the only known predators of barracuda are sharks, tuna, and huge grouper. Adult barracuda—which, by the way, can live to be fourteen or older—are capable of great bursts of speed, and can swim perhaps as fast at forty miles per hour over short distances. Barracuda are highly attuned to the struggling of injured fish (and blood in the water) and may appear seemingly out of nowhere to investigate a possible meal. If you've got a large tattoo of a fish on your rear end, you'd better watch your ass.

Most scuba divers report that barracuda are more curious than threatening, and these inquisitive fish may follow a swimmer or diver some distance before turning away. The good news is that an attack on a human is likely to consist of a single, painful bite, after which the barracuda will probably swim away when it realizes you are not another fish. The bad news is that the bite can be large and leave permanent scarring. And, like most predatory fish, the barracuda is attracted to shiny objects that reflect sunlight, mimicking the gills of a fish. Ankle and charm bracelets hanging over the side of your inner tube are asking for trouble.

Or Portuguese man-of-war?

OK, so the Portuguese man-of-war (sometimes called a bluebottle because of its bluish-purplish color) isn't *really* a jellyfish. It's actually a *siphonophore*, which means it's several different organisms living and working together—to get you! (Not really; they don't actively seek out prey.) These huge creatures—their tentacles may reach 160 feet or more—are carnivores, and their tentacles are exceedingly poisonous. They also congregate in large groups, with numbers sometimes reaching into the thousands. If you see one near your inner tube, it may be too late to escape. At least it's not Jaws.

Most likely, you'll spot the *pneumatophore*, or gas-filled bladder, first. It's about a foot long, and it floats. It can catch the breeze like a sail, enabling the creature (which has no means of self-propulsion) to move. Streaming downward off the pneumatophore are the tentacles (the second of four organisms), which are covered with toxic nematocysts. These venom-filled "stingers" trap fish and paralyze them. For a human, just brushing up against a tentacle is incredibly painful, and the discomfort may persist for days. A sting will start with intense localized pain, followed by aching joints, redness, and lesions. In severe cases, scarring isn't unusual, and people with allergies may develop life-threatening complications. Some claim pain at the sting site can return months or even years after contact with a bluebottle, though this may be apocryphal. Regardless, the tentacles are very dangerous and even contact with a dead man-of-war will cause a reaction. Tentacles separated from the man-of-war body are equally dangerous as those still attached, so don't play "wave that tentacle" on the beach.

After catching and killing its prey, muscles in the man-of-war's tentacles will pass the victim (you?) up to special polyps that contain the third organism, which breaks down and digests prey. (A fourth section has the reproductive organs.)

For a seemingly complex organism, the man-of-war is not as intelligent as a barracuda. The pneumatophore will deflate to escape potential threats on the surface (and may inflate or deflate

CHOICE BITS

* While not a typical game fish, a barracuda will put up a fight when caught on a line, and its flesh can be eaten—though it carries the risk of ciguatera poisoning.

* Putting vinegar (or urine) on a man-of-war sting will do nothing to reduce pain and may actually make things worse.

* Never touch pieces of a man-of-war tentacle with your bare hands; use a rubber glove or a piece of driftwood to remove any remaining parts.

* Man-of-wars are hermaphrodites.

to catch the wind), and the tentacles will quickly envelop prey, but otherwise the creature simply drifts with the winds and the tides. Thus, spotting a man-of-war near your inner tube doesn't mean you are actively being hunted. But it does mean the dangerous tentacles are in the water around you. Fortunately, man-of-wars are usually only seen near beaches when strong onshore breezes push them toward land from the open ocean.

Sharp teeth or stinging tendrils? Six-foot or 160-foot predator? Barracuda or bluebottle? Hey, it could be worse. You could spot both.

They travel in dangerous groups of twenty or more. They're almost always found near ranchers and cowboys. States are busy passing laws in an attempt to control them. And they are indiscriminate killers, randomly striking down some individuals while leaving others unscathed. Yes, wolves and cigarettes are perhaps more alike than different—though cattle are not typically felled by emphysema. But which one would be worse to face, week after week: A pack of Luckies or a pack of gray wolves? Either way, you'd better have a good health plan.

Environmentalists defend their right to roam the West. Ranchers call them a nuisance at best, killers at worst. You'll have plenty of time to make your own decision as you face down a hungry pack of wolves once a week, every week, for the rest of your days (which may be numbered). How's, say, Tuesday for you? Does Tuesday work?

The *Dances with Wolves* image of the solitary gray wolf roaming the landscape is fiction. Wolves almost always live and hunt in groups ("packs"), and most of the individuals in the pack are related. A pack can be anywhere from two to fifteen wolves (four to seven is common) though two packs may combine into a very large group. The so-called alpha wolf, the most confident (and sometimes strongest) of the group, is the leader of the pack, and all other animals are submissive to him or her. Wolves are intensely territorial, and will defend their land vigorously, especially from stray wolves that are not pack members. Unfortunately, you chose the wrong spot to build your log cabin.

On the first Tuesday of the month, the wolves will begin nosing around your property. The howling will start early in the morning, both as a way to communicate with other animals in the pack and to signal the beginning of the hunt. (The howl may be audible for ten miles.) Wolves are entirely comfortable attacking large mammals, especially deer, bison, elk, and moose: they hunt in packs because they require numbers to injure and kill their large prey. While it's true that wolves rarely attack humans unless provoked, your habit of hand-feeding them your table scraps was never a good policy from the start. Now, accustomed to your presence, the wolves are more likely to attack.

The wolves will begin Tuesday's attack by chasing you until you tire, perhaps into deep snow or ice where you will become trapped or lose your footing. The attack will probably not be accompanied by growling/snarling/snapping, but more ominously will be intensely quiet. Attacks will come quickly and be aimed at your legs and feet, with the intention of hobbling you and bringing you down. After that, one or several wolves will go for the jugular, and then the party begins. *A-wooo!*

Like all animals, wolves are fearful of fire, so swinging a torch to frighten off the lead attacker may deter that wolf and the rest of the pack from following through with the attack. Yelling or throwing rocks may also serve to deter an attack. Or you could run inside and shut the door. Once you've frustrated the attack and the wolves realize they have failed, they will slink off in search of new prey. Until next week, when it all begins again.

Or pack of cigarettes?

They always travel in large numbers (packs), they show up when you're at your most stressed and vulnerable, and their filter tips offer a false sense of security. They are killers, and they insidiously relax and calm you while secretly shaving years off your life. A pack of smokes once a week, for the rest of your life. However shortened it may be.

Like a wolf pack, an already-dangerous group of cigarettes may combine with other packs to form an especially deadly "carton," readily available at any corner grocery. The most vulnerable individuals in the carton, the "soft packs," can be easily crushed or broken, resulting in an additional cash outlay to purchase the more robust "hard packs." These cigarettes are virtually indestructible, and attacking them with open flame only makes them more perilous. The most deadly of all cigarettes are the "alpha smokes," the so-called 100s. These extra-large specimens will hang around longer and produce vast quantities of carcinogens before finally dying out and being replaced by a new member of the pack.

Cigarettes also emit a deadly cloud of smoke, attacking any individuals around you and leaving them coughing and gasping for air. Highly dangerous "smoking circles" or "smokers' groups" congregate around the entrances of buildings, beckoning you with camaraderie, tall tales of "smokers' rights," and a hazy, stinking premise of solidarity in the face of crushing societal pressure to quit. It's the siren song of the cigarette pack, and it is very difficult to resist.

A pack-a-week habit will cost you roughly $240 per year—less if you live in North Carolina, which has the nation's lowest cigarette tax. But in terms of your long-term health, the price is likely to be much higher: twice the risk of heart attack; twenty-three times the risk of lung cancer for men (thirteen times the risk for women); twelve times the risk of chronic obstructive pulmonary disease for men and thirteen times the risk for women. Overall, tobacco use is the single most avoidable cause of disease, disability, and death in the United States. A pack of wolves scratching at your door may seem more dangerous, but a pack of cigarettes in your back pocket may actually be much worse. Especially if you tend to smoke in bed.

Pack of wolves or pack of cigarettes. Yes, you may survive this week's wolf attack, but what about next week's? And this week's pack of cigarettes? Well, it's going to be your last. Sure it is. No, it really is, you mean it this time. If you fight them off long enough, the wolves may eventually become extinct. On the other hand, if you smoke long enough, so will you.

It starts with a quiet shuffling, a rustling among the leaves and the trees. Shadows dance across the tent wall, darting this way and that. Is that a tail, or a bandana? Soon you hear footsteps getting closer, and an odd smell—an animal scent, maybe, or a mixture of sweat and dirt—drifts into the tent. Peeking outside, you recoil in fright as you spot . . . rats, or Rambo. It's another tough choice: vermin or an angry Vietnam vet out for revenge?

Rats . . .

The Norway rat (*Rattus norvegicus*, also known as the brown rat or "sewer rat") isn't exactly man's best friend. Large, aggressive, destructive, capable of eating pretty much anything and getting into pretty much anywhere—wait, isn't that Rambo, too?—rats carry disease and are found almost everywhere on the planet. Rats outside your tent could mean you've accidentally pitched it on a rat hole. Or a landfill.

Rats are generally considered the most widespread terrestrial mammal, partly because they reproduce prodigiously: females give birth less than a month after mating; the average litter has at least six baby rats; and females have four to six litters per year. That's a lot of rats, and they're ready to breed just three months after birth. Rats are also fiercely territorial and will attack interlopers (especially other rats, Rambo, and you) if their living space is invaded. Rats love to dig and chew, have excellent senses of smell and hearing, and are great swimmers (both on the surface and underwater). Spotting rats outside your tent probably means you've brought along some of their favorite meals: cereal, scrambled eggs, and macaroni. You would've been better off bringing a dinner of celery, raw beets, and a few peaches—their least favorite foods. Of course, a very hungry rat will eat anything.

Rats are typically not shy around humans, though, because they are nocturnal, may wait until you are asleep to chew their way into your tent (or burrow up from below) to get at your foodstuffs. If you have not sufficiently washed your hands, they may also chew on your fingers. Though the common sewer rat does not carry plague, you may be exposed to a raft of other dangerous diseases, including Weil's disease, cryptosporidiosis, viral hemorrhagic fever, and hantavirus pulmonary syndrome. Not to mention the old standbys, fleas, ticks, and lice. Where there's one rat, there are always more rats, since they live in large groups (clans) with extended family members, including multiple sexually active females. Bringing along the family cat or dog is not likely to scare a determined rat. And, in fact, the rat will probably go after your pet's food when it falls asleep. Or your pet.

Or Rambo?

They sent him on a mission and set him up to fail. But they made one mistake. They forgot they were dealing with Rambo.

He'll go anywhere, eat anything, dig his way to safety, and destroy whatever he finds. He can't be trapped, and he can't be stopped. But he's not a rat, he's a vet. He's John J. Rambo (aka Sylvester Stallone), a loner just looking for a hot meal, some old Army buddies, and an M-60 belt-fed machine gun. Did you happen to bring yours?

Rambo doesn't like rats. He doesn't like sheriffs, either. Or sheriff's deputies. Or things that remind him of the 'Nam. Like your pup tent. Rambo is an expert tracker, so he'll have little trouble locating your campsite. He'll approach quietly, flat on his belly, just like he was trained to do in the Special Forces. He'll wait until you're asleep, then use his Bowie knife to cut his way in. Or he may simply kick over the whole tent, jump you, and put the knife to your throat. And you were worried about bears!

The good news is that Rambo typically won't kill civilians. The bad news is that you recently joined the National Guard and this is your "one weekend a month." In a fair fight, you'll probably stand little chance against Rambo. During a recent trip to Afghanistan, Rambo single-handedly killed 108 men. On another excursion, to rescue POWs in Vietnam, he killed 61 (two more

⚖ CHOICE BITS

* A Norwegian rat may be eighteen inches long.

* When injured or weak rats die off or are killed, the remaining clan members will increase their reproduction rate to compensate.

* In 1985, *Rambo: First Blood Part II* won numerous "Golden Raspberry" awards, including "Worst Picture"; "Worst Original Song" ("Peace in Our Life"); "Worst Screenplay" (Stallone and James Cameron); and "Worst Actor" (Stallone). It was the second-highest grossing film of the year, after *Back to the Future*.

kills than his entire tour in Vietnam!). You may be able to catch a break by claiming that you were "in country," but be prepared to be questioned about your unit and where you served. Wrong answers will be dealt with harshly. Rambo also enjoys blowing stuff up, so hide your camping stove. If all else fails, get Colonel Trautman on the phone to talk some sense into the man.

Rats or Rambo? Tough choices don't get much tougher than this one. The rats have the numbers, but John J. Rambo's got the skills. And the chip on his shoulder.

WHICH WOULD BE WORSE TO WAKE UP TO, VAMPIRE BATS OR HOOKWORMS?

Some choices are like beds: things are much easier if they're left unmade. But in this case, falling asleep might be difficult if you know you'll wake up with killer creatures ready to feed on your blood. Mosquitoes can be swatted, and leeches can be plucked off. But bats and hookworms present a whole new range of challenges—along with the requisite health dangers. So before you crawl into bed, it's time to choose who you'd like crawling in with you: vampire bats or hookworms? The bed bugs have the night off.

No, they don't actually turn into vampires (or vice versa). And they don't turn you into a vampire, either. Or a bat. But a single bite could turn you into a raving lunatic, should the bat be carrying disease. Some have even speculated that disease transmission from vampire bats to humans was responsible for the "vampire" myths of yore. (Though this is doubtful; see the "Werewolf vs. Dracula" section for a more plausible explanation.) Still, vampire bats are dangerous and destructive creatures with a taste for (and only for) blood. You did throw the extra blanket on, right?

Vampire bats (of which there are actually three distinct types) require mammalian blood to live; if they don't get a good dose every few days they will die. Vampire bats feed exclusively at night, so there's little chance you'll wake up to one perched on your monitor during a nap at your desk—unless you work nights. Once the sun goes down, however, vampire bats will emerge by the thousands from their homes, typically very dark places like caves, wells, mines, and so on. Unlike all other types of bats, they will avoid both fruit and insects and instead concentrate on their favorite meals: the blood of cows, pigs, birds, and horses. Scientists believe that vampire bats prefer the blood of these animals to the taste of human blood, but the creatures can and will sup on human blood if no other options are present.

Could you actually wake up to find a bat feeding on your leg? Yes, but only if you're lucky enough to wake up. Vampire bats typically feed late at night, because that's when their "donors" are

153

KILLER CREATURES

asleep. And, unlike other bats, they are very skilled at walking and jumping (and even running!), allowing them to creep up very stealthily on their prey instead of landing on it from above, an action that could wake the victim. Vampire bats are also small and light, and use a special heat receptor to locate their warm-blooded meals. When a bat lands, it uses its very sharp front teeth to prick two tiny punctures in the skin. The bat's saliva contains *draculin* (sound familiar?), an anticoagulant that keeps the victim's blood flowing. Once there's a steady stream, the bat actually licks (or laps up) the blood, rather than sucking it—again, probably so as not to wake the donor. That tickling at your toes? That's not the family dog.

Typically, a bat will eat/drink about a tablespoon of blood at each meal, though vampire bats have been observed feeding for thirty minutes or more on heavy sleepers. Sometimes, a bat will consume so much blood that it's unable to coax its woozy, engorged body to fly, forcing it to walk or jump to a safe location. The good news is that as long as their preferred meals are present, vampire bats will avoid biting and feeding on humans. The bad news is that bats are the world's most common carrier of rabies, the debilitating neurological disease for which there is no cure once symptoms arrive—and a vampire bat's bite is so small that you probably won't even notice it. On the other hand, vampire bats are said to be highly intelligent and very tame, and some have even been trained to come when someone calls their names (*Count? Bitey?*). Vampire bats are also very social, and a satiated bat may regurgitate blood into the mouth of a hungry bat that can't find a meal. Supposedly, this looks like kissing. How sweet!

Or hookworms?

As far as blood-sucking animals go, vampire bats probably take the cake—as long as it's got blood frosting. But when it comes to nasty intestinal parasites that feed on human blood, hookworms are the definite frontrunner. True, they don't carry rabies, but jeez, wouldn't you rather wake up to pancakes?

Hookworms are a dangerous parasite with a complex life cycle, and are very common in many parts of the world; it's been estimated that nearly one billion people are infected. Hookworm has been called a disease of poverty because walking on contaminated soil in bare feet can result in infection through the soles of the feet (though you can be infected by ingesting contaminated soil or food, too). Tiny worm larvae burrow through the skin and enter the bloodstream, eventually reaching the mouth, where they are swallowed. After about a week, the larvae reach the small intestine and attach themselves to the intestinal wall, where they feed on blood as they mature into half-inch-long adult worms. The adults lay thousands of eggs which are passed out of the body in the stool; the stool makes its way into soil; and the larvae hatch and the cycle begins anew.

Waking up to an infection—*the early bird gets the worm!*— would probably mean noticing an itchy rash on the soles of your feet. A serious infection would most likely be accompanied by abdominal pain, loss of appetite, and diarrhea. However, an initially minor infection might have no symptoms at all. Once the hookworms attach to the intestine and begin feeding, though, major complications can ensue, including anemia, difficulty

CHOICE BITS

* Vampire bat saliva has been used effectively in anticlotting medication for stroke victims.

* Male vampire bats may have a "harem" of twenty female breeding partners.

* Female vampire bats typically have only one offspring at a time.

* Hookworms may stay in the small intestine for years.

breathing, irregular heartbeat, and even death. Those blood-thirsty kissing bats are looking better and better!

Hookworm is typically present in tropical and subtropical areas, places where a frost does not interrupt the part of the hookworm life cycle that occurs outside the human body. The good news is that infection in the Unites States is rare (but, then, so are vampire bats), and in any case infection can be easily treated with single dose of a drug called *albendazole*. And, of course, wearing shoes and washing hands after touching soil are easy prevention measures. Still, how gross.

Another day, another blood-sucking organism to contend with. But which one? They're both bad, but which one is worse? And can you sleep with one eye open?

No one ever said bringing a new pet into the family was easy. There's the scratching at the furniture, the unwelcome 5:00 a.m. licking of your face, and the always pleasant clean-up and disposal of the pet waste. And all that vacuuming! They say fish are pets for people who don't like pets, and lizards are for people who don't like fish. But what if your fish and your lizard are, um, not house broken? It's time to lay out the newspaper—you're going to need several Sundays' worth—as you choose either Jaws or Godzilla to bring home to the family. You may need a bigger pet carrier.

And people think pit bulls have a bad reputation . . . poor Jaws has been waiting years for adoption. He's been biding his time, swimming in slow, deliberate circles, just waiting for a good home. Now, he's finally found it: your swimming pool. Think about rescheduling that pool party.

Sharks like Jaws prefer open water to being confined in a small space, so there might be some initial resentment at being penned in. Like all pets, Jaws may take out his frustrations with misbehavior, including snapping at family members, chewing on household items, and eating the pool boy. However, after several days "Jawsy" will probably become accustomed to his new home and his vivacious, energetic personality will return. His newfound comfort level will be noticeable when you enter the pool and feel him "bump" or "rub" up against you. He may even exhibit "chasing" behavior, where he swims after you and slams you playfully with his snout. Be cautious, however, as sharks have skin the texture of sandpaper and even a brief encounter may leave you scraped and bleeding.

A word about keeping sharks as pets: typical aquarium species include nurse sharks, black tip reef sharks, epaulette sharks, leopard sharks and horn sharks. Great whites demand constant care, attention, and, especially, feeding. In fact, a bucket of chum every few days is not likely to keep Jaws from wanting to snack between meals. And while he must constantly swim or he'll die, that doesn't mean he's getting enough exercise. One way to keep him active is to enter your pool in a rowboat and play "chase," a game where you row as fast as you possibly can and Jaws swims very quickly behind you. Try dangling a foot out of the boat for even more excitement.

As with introducing any new pet to your home, take precautions to avoid conflicts between Jaws and youngsters, as well as any existing pets. Sharks *love* small children, and kids splashing around in water wings and "floaties" will excite Jaws to no end. However, when hungry he tends to play rough and may try to devour them. Similarly, the family cat or dog should be kept well back from the pool edge to avoid a nasty surprise and clogs in the filter. On the bright side, when Jaws catches his prey he's unlikely to leave a dead "present" for you somewhere in the house. Unlike a dog, Jaws will not allow himself to be caged at any time. You, on the other hand, should always be in a cage when you enter the pool. Keep a speargun handy, too.

Or Godzilla?

Yes, they are cold-blooded and not especially cuddly. And yes, they will only attack and eat live prey, which can be a major hassle. But lizards—even giant, radiation-modified, man-eating ones like Godzilla—can be pleasant around the house, with the proper precautions. As a first step, consider removing the roof.

Godzilla (or *Gojira*, as he prefers to be called) can be, like any lizard, a wild and unpredictable creature. To make matters worse, Godzilla is at least 150 feet tall and twenty thousand tons, making a terrarium for him an unlikely home. Instead, consider allowing Godzilla to roam about the house freely, but with proper supervision (and keep doors and windows closed). Fragile objects such as glassware, china, and children should be placed out of harm's way, like in another town. Also, keep in mind that, unlike normal lizards, Godzilla is fire-breathing and carries a danger of immolation. On the bright side, you can throw out the barbecue. (On occasion, and depending on his diet, Godzilla may also have "atomic breath" which cannot be eliminated with chewable treats.)

Godzilla will probably not get on well with your other pets and should be chosen over Jaws only if he'll be in a cat-and-dog-free environment. Along these lines, cleaning up after the "king of the monsters" is going to be a royal pain, and will require a backhoe, dump truck, and lots of Lysol. Also, take care to avoid bringing Godzilla into a suburban environment where nearby houses may be home to the beasts Mothra, Baragon, and King Ghidorah. A shock collar will not prevent 'Zilla from wandering into neighboring yards and laying waste to all he encounters.

Like some lizards and salamanders, Godzilla also has impressive powers of regeneration: if he, say, gets the tip of his tail caught in a doorway, he'll simply grow another one without a problem. Though he will stay on land for long periods, Godzilla prefers to live underwater and may try to escape from your home to a nearby golf course with a suitably large water hazard. Should this happen, clear the course and try to coax him out with a can of tuna.

Finally, a note about his longevity. Like all lizards, Godzilla may live for many years in captivity. However, as he grows older and begins to limit his movement, he may become sick and need to be "put down." The only effective means for doing so is blasting him with Dr. Serizawa's oxygen destroyer, which will overcome his regenerative powers by dissolving him down to the bone, and then turning him to dust. Say your good-byes and then leave; do not be present during the euthanasia process.

They say people with pets are happier, less stressed, and live longer, healthier lives. You'll be the exception to the rule. But which pet will it be, Jaws or Godzilla? No matter which one you choose, make sure it doesn't mate.

WHICH WOULD YOU RATHER HAVE AS A BREAKFAST CEREAL, HARVESTER ANTS OR RATTLESNAKES?

S o, you think you're a morning person? You may take up sleeping in when you see what's set out next to your bagel and cream cheese: a big bowl of danger, with a little skim milk. Remember how, as a kid, your parents wouldn't let you have sugary cereal? It would rot your teeth out, they said. Well, cavities are going to be the least of your worries as you plow into your teeming helping of Critter Crunch. But which deadly creature do you prefer, harvester ants or rattlesnakes? And they said Lucky Charms were bad for you . . .

Harvester ants . . .

Don't worry, "Morning Harvester" cereal is completely organic. So organic, in fact, that it's simply *alive* with flavor. And danger.

In fact, you might want to *add* poisonous chemicals to this meal. Just don't sprinkle the bowl with sugar.

Harvester ants are dangerous insects that have been termed "warlike." They will not hesitate to swarm and sting any perceived threat to their nest or queen, including insects, humans, and even other ants. They are big (up to half an inch long) and orange to red to reddish brown—though you're not likely to mistake them for Frosted Flakes. Typically, harvester ants like to eat seeds, so they may make a run at your sesame bagel. But they have been known to attack and eat insects if they've exhausted their natural food supply. The ants also don't like shade, and so will remove any foliage around their colony (watch how they denude your centerpiece). They have very strong jaws which are used to bite and crack open the seeds that they horde.

When harvester ants sting they sting repeatedly and viciously, and multiple stings can kill (especially people who are allergic). The sting site first swells and turns red, and these symptoms are followed by a throbbing pain that may last hours or days. The area around the bite may become moist and/or sticky. After being poured out of the box and into your cereal bowl, the ants will probably be momentarily confused, and several workers will scramble up your spoon—leaving a chemical scent for others to follow—as they seek escape. The ants will quickly swarm onto your hand and arm, and will most likely begin biting when they feel threatened or confused. Consider attempting to drown the ants: whole milk is thicker and will work better than skim. The box may contain a prize (perhaps the queen), but sticking your arm in to retrieve it is not recommended.

CHOICE BITS

❋ Chocolate-covered ants are high in protein, but typically only black ants are used (and they are not eaten while alive).

❋ Some harvester ants have wings and can fly.

❋ There are dozens of species of rattlesnake; the Mojave rattlesnake is the most poisonous and is never used in cereal.

❋ Rattlesnakes will continue to grow replacement fangs as long as they live.

=== **Or rattlesnakes?** ===

Along with milk, juice, toast, and spread, it's a complete breakfast—completely poisonous, that is, and not especially appetizing. *Snakes on a Plane* may be pretty scary, but rattlers in you cereal bowl isn't exactly Wheaties, either. Do not shake the box before serving.

First, the good. Rattlesnakes are not especially aggressive, and usually will only strike when they feel threatened—or are poured out of a cereal box. Though rattlesnakes won't always vibrate their tails (rattles) before they strike—and they can strike from a noncoiled position—a bowl of coiled, noisy snakes is not a particularly safe breakfast. Rattlesnakes can also bite while submerged, so trying to drown them in milk probably won't work. (Also, when the rattles get wet they may not make noise.) Like spaghetti, snakes also tend to fall off the spoon, so you may need a long fork if you plan to enjoy them before work or school.

Rattlesnakes inject a dangerous hemotoxic venom that destroys tissue and organs and disrupts blood clotting. The good news is that rattlers don't always inject venom when they bite. The bad news is that when they do, it's considered a medical emergency and requires a speedy trip to the hospital to get antivenin administered. Untreated (or untimely treated) venomous bites are usually fatal. Even a snack-size "kiddie" cereal box filled with baby rattlesnakes is dangerous, since baby rattlers are born with functional fangs and strong venom.

Like instant oatmeal, rattlesnake cereal is best eaten cooked. Assuming you can catch the snakes and avoid being bitten, just chop the heads off, skin them, and roast the flesh: the meat is chewy and tastes like chicken—though it's probably most appropriate as a dinner entrée. (Remember, rattlesnakes aren't just for breakfast anymore.) Or, consider keeping the snakes as pets.

Forget snap, crackle, and pop. This day will start with crawl, sting, and bite. But which box to choose, "Morning Harvester" (*Now with 30% More Ants!*) or "Rise-n-Rattle" (*Double Venom!*)? Might want to send the kids to school without breakfast.

PART FIVE

PERILOUS PLACES

No one ever claimed being a chef was easy. The long hours on your feet, the pressure-packed work environment, that pesky health department—they're all conspiring against you. Sometimes you'd like nothing more than to lie down, relax, and get a good massage. Well, sure, but who wouldn't? Instead you get to peel seventy-five pounds of potatoes. And then it's time to sharpen those knives and plug in the meat grinder—don't back into it or you'll get behind in your orders—for a few hours of either chopping onions or making sausage. But which is worse? The onions will have you in tears, but today is blood sausage day. And you're a vegetarian.

The ski goggles are in place. You're chewing a piece of bread. And you're holding a lit match between your teeth (while chewing, no easy feat). It's all in a (vain) attempt to avoid the most tear-jerking of all vegetables: the papery tiger, the layered lion, the white shark. The dreaded onion. Did you notice tonight's specials? Onion soup and onion rings.

Ask ten chefs how to avoid crying while chopping onions and you'll get ten different answers. Some claim chopping the onions on a cutting board just above (or below) an exhaust fan will do the trick, or cutting them under running water. Some chefs breathe through their mouths, while others swear by keeping their mouths shut. Other experts keep a burner going on the stove. One well-known chef famously did all his chopping in a walk-in fridge, while another used a portable oxygen tank, an electric carving knife, and three shiny copper pennies (don't ask). Some chefs will simply relegate the task to their sous chefs. But what if you're the sous chef?

While there is some truth (and moderate effectiveness) to most of these "cures," they tend to be more complex than necessary. Chopping onions releases sulfur enzymes trapped in the flesh of the onion. The "gas" floats up to your face and your eyes begin to tear in a vain attempt to wash away the invader. The more you chop, the more gas is released and the more you cry. (Incidentally, shallots and the white parts of scallions are also tear-inducing, though they are smaller and have lower sulfur levels. Onion soup mix is safe.)

Most of the sulfur is trapped in the root (the "hairy part") of the onion, so avoiding chopping this section provides some relief. One trick that seems to work is storing the onions in the refrigerator (*not* on the counter.) The chilling effect reduces the amount of gas released when the onion is chopped. (If the onions were stored on the counter, place them in the freezer for about ten minutes before chopping.) Another trick is to use a very sharp knife, which cuts but doesn't "crush" the cells of the onion, releasing less gas—plus, the chopping will go faster. Don't attempt to chop the onions with a butter knife or a spoon.

What if you're being punished/tortured and you're sentenced to chop ten twenty-pound bags of onions that you can't refrigerate or freeze, and you have no access to the other dubious methods? You could try growing longer arms, but that could take years. A better method is sitting right there on the counter in front of you: the food processor. It's an effective (and quick) way to dice lots of onions. Stand *way* back when you take the lid off.

Or making sausage?

The old saying goes that sausages are like laws: it's best not to see them being made. (Or maybe it's the other way around. But the point's the same.) But what if you not only have to see them made, but make them yourself? If it's true that everything from the pig but the squeal goes into sausage, it's not going to be pretty. Pretty or not, though, it's time to get your intestines in a row and start stuffing.

Start out with *boudin noir*, or blood sausage. You'll need pork fatback, pork casing, ground pork, garlic, parsley, apple, milk, nutmeg, black pepper, and (of course) a pint of *very* fresh pig's blood. You can bleed the pig yourself, but remember to continuously move a foreleg to keep the blood flowing and avoid clots. Stir the warm blood to keep it from coagulating, or use a centrifuge. Using your hands, mix all the ingredients together. Make sure the warm blood is evenly distributed in the bowl. Do not lick your fingers. Slide the casing onto the end of a funnel and pour the bloody liquid mixture into the top. Tie off the casing and drop the sausage into boiling water. Boil for about twenty minutes. Open the windows to help the vile odor dissipate. Refrigerate the sausage, wash your hands for about two hours, and you're done!

Perhaps making haggis, Scotland's favorite dish, is preferable to blood sausage? For this meal, you'll need: one sheep lung (illegal in the Unites States, so you'll need to slaughter the sheep yourself); one sheep stomach; one sheep heart; one sheep liver; half pound of suet (mutton fat, found around the kidneys); oatmeal; and spices. First, wash the stomach and the lungs well, cover with cold water, and soak for several hours. You'll also need to turn the stomach inside out. Next, boil the heart and liver, remove from water, then chop the heart and grate the liver with a coarse cheese grater. Sauté the oatmeal until golden, combine with other ingredients, and stuff the mixture into the stomach and lungs with your hands—leave some room or when the oatmeal expands the stomach will burst!—and truss with kitchen string. Boil for about three hours, remove from water, and place on a platter with a spoon. Serve the haggis with "neeps, tatties, and nips": mashed turnips, mashed potatoes, and nips of whiskey. Lots and lots of nips. Like, the whole bottle.

Chopping onions or making sausage? Vegetarians might prefer chopping onions, but meat eaters may embrace their inner vegetarian after making sausage. One wrinkle: sausage recipes usually call for chopped onion.

WHICH WOULD BE WORSE, LUNCH AT NEVERLAND RANCH OR BREAKFAST AT A POULTRY-PROCESSING PLANT?

Some places are dangerous. Some places are creepy. The worst places are dangerous, creepy, *and* secretive. After all, if they're trying to keep you out, there must be a pretty good reason for doing so, some sort of alarming mysteries that could inflame public opinion should they leak out. But the veil of secrecy is going to be lifted just this once, for your visit to either Michael Jackson's Neverland Ranch or a large poultry-processing facility churning out chickens. You may want to bring a surgical mask.

Lunch at Neverland . . .

Welcome to the most disturbing afternoon of your life. The gates to Michael's 2,800-acre Shangri-la in the mountains of Santa

Barbara county swing open and beckon you to a child's fantasy land—or anyway what a full-grown man with children of his own fantasizes a child would fantasize about. You've decided against bringing your ten-year-old nephew along, despite the invitation, so you can get the lay of the land first. But, as instructed, you have brought your coloring book, stuffed animals, and Hot Wheels.

You will probably be picked up at the gates in a golf cart by a member of M.J.'s elite security squad, the Office of Special Security (or, at least, by a member who does not have a lawsuit against Michael still pending). Because Michael is no longer a full-time resident at Neverland you may notice things falling into disrepair, giving the ranch the feeling of a deserted amusement park fallen on hard times, a Disneyland gone to seed. The Ferris wheel is rusted and creaking in the breeze, the horses on the merry-go-round shedding flakes of paint and cracking from sun exposure. The mini-railway looks as if bandits have blown the tracks, and the asphalt of the go-kart speedway is potholed, the mini-racecars sporting flat tires and leaking oil.

On the way to the mansion, you'll speed by the decrepit Neverland zoo, the forlorn animals hoping for adoption (but not by Mike Tyson). The smell of charred foliage will fill the air, the result of a 2006 wildfire that burned forty acres of the ranch and almost took out the main house. The house itself is in serious disrepair—nothing like it was for the lifelong union of Liz Taylor to Larry Fortensky in 1991. (Now *that* was a party!) Still, Michael will be flying in from Bahrain to join you for the standard Neverland lunch of hot dogs, mac and cheese, McDonald's Happy Meals, and, for dessert, ice cream sundaes and cotton candy. While you wait, you'll be able to play video games, jump up and down on the moon bounce (don't forget to remove your shoes!), and peruse Michael's large collection of glossy magazines. Oddly, there are no pictures at Neverland of Michael as a little boy. They must have gotten lost during the move.

Michael, in sunglasses, fedora, and desert-chic caftan, will sweep in with his entourage and offer you a drink, perhaps his famous "jungle juice," which may leave you feeling a bit woozy. However, seeing that you've arrived alone he may get perturbed and leave the table to sulk, perhaps going for a timeout in "Macaulay's room." Once on Michael's bad side, you may be escorted off the premises and left at the gate. You should be able to catch a ride back to town with one of photographers staked out there.

Or breakfast at a poultry-processing plant?

If you think chicken comes in one of two forms, nuggets or shrink-wrapped, you're in for a long morning. Should you shun Neverland you'll pay a visit to one of the nation's most perilous work places, a factory where the term "free range" means someone just won a stove. You'll be exposed to the sights, sounds, and smells of modern industrial meat processing and packing, in all its low-wage glory. Oh, and breakfast today is fried eggs and chicken sausage.

Poultry slaughtering and processing plants have among the highest rates of workplace injury in the nation, including lacerations, repetitive trauma (carpal tunnel, bursitis, noise-induced hearing loss), infection, and long-term illness. In fact, poultry processing injury and illness rates are one and a half times the average for manufacturing and more than double the rate for private industry as a whole. As you munch on your sausage, note that much of the poultry-processing industry is still not automated, with workers cutting carcasses manually as the slaughtered birds move down an assembly line.

You may want to consider enjoying your eggs in the break room and not on the factory floor, since fecal contamination at the plant is of particular concern, especially occupational exposure to *psittacosis*, a bacterial infection caused by the inhalation of infected particles from bird droppings. Symptoms begin one to three weeks after exposure, and usually include headache, fever, and cough. Flulike symptoms of nausea/vomiting and joint/muscle aches are also common, and severe infection can develop into pneumonia. You'll still be better off than the chicken, however.

Watching the assembly (or, more accurately, disassembly) line, you may be tempted to lend a hand—though hopefully not literally, as workplace amputations are common. If so, you'll be very low on the pecking order: you will face a twelve-hour shift, wages that have been stagnant since 1979, and cutting motions that you'll repeat at least ten thousand (and perhaps forty thousand) times per shift. You'll process 190 birds an hour, on average, and may be forced to work through your break. You also won't be paid for the time it takes to put on and take off your protective gear. (That's "your time.") If you have kids, you'll qualify for food stamps, the national school lunch program, and the Low-Income Home Energy Assistance Program (LIHEAP).

The good news? Though the work is very difficult, if you keep at it you may reap the benefits of one of the numerous

🏛️ CHOICE BITS

* Estimates of the value of Neverland (or at least the land there) range from about $12 million (Santa Barbara County Assessor's Office) to many times that (*Forbes*).

* A jukebox in the kids' arcade at Neverland concealed a wine cellar.

* Chicken is the most popular meat in the United States.

class-action lawsuits filed against the poultry-processing industry by workers' groups. These suits are typically settled for millions.

Lunch with the King of Pop or breakfast among the five-pound broilers? A few hours at either place is likely to make you ill. On the other hand you can always sue and hope for a big settlement. It's worked before.

WHICH WOULD BE WORSE, VISITING NORTH KOREA WITH GERALDO RIVERA OR GETTING TRAPPED AMONG THE DONNERS WITH JOAN RIVERS?

North Korea and the Donner Pass should both be pretty high on the list of places you'd rather not be: the former is a nuclear-armed, outlaw regime run by a madman and the latter perhaps the most infamous case of cannibalism in history. But bad can always get worse, and things could really go downhill fast if you were accompanied by Geraldo or Joan, two "personalities" who never met an audience they didn't like. So roll the dice and then roll the cameras. Everyone with nothing better to do is watching.

North Korea with Geraldo . . .

Many people forget that Geraldo made his television bones with a powerful, Emmy-winning 1972 report about sexual abuse in a

New York State school for retarded children. Instead, they recall the man whom *Newsweek* dubbed the king of "Trash TV" with *The Geraldo Rivera Show*, the talk-show model for Jerry Springer (and many others) that featured cross-dressers, battling skinheads, and Satanists. Geraldo loves the action—his nose was once broken in a fight and he had plastic surgery, both on camera—and would like nothing more than to accompany you on your trip to Pyongyang to meet Kim Jong Il, North Korea's "Dear Leader." Prepare for an international incident.

Poor, starving, and isolated, North Korea has played the nuclear card, the only one it has left. Geraldo would certainly insist that you track down the country's nuclear weapons testing site, promising viewers "shocking, exclusive" footage of North Korea's fissile material. You would first don bulky, lead-lined suits and, carrying Geiger counters and dosimeters and accompanied by nuclear-weapons experts and Army personnel, make an arduous ascent to a remote mountain range where Geraldo, after an interminable countdown, would swing open a thick vault set into concrete to find . . . well, probably nothing. Undaunted, and with an audience of thirty million, Geraldo would claim the North Koreans had been "tipped off" (possibly by the weeks of advertising for the show), provoking a declaration of war from Dear Leader and a missile strike on South Korea. You would all go to prison.

Or, things could go a different way. Geraldo might accompany you on a clandestine mission to cross the heavily fortified border between North and South Korea. With cameras rolling, he might describe to the audience the top-secret details of the incursion, perhaps drawing a map of your exact position in the sand. An avid fan of popular culture, Kim Jong Il would view the broadcast, provoking a declaration of war and a missile strike on South Korea. You would all go to prison.

Or, Geraldo could accompany you on a state-sponsored visit to Kim Jong Il and insist on an interview. After the interview, Geraldo would insist he was convinced that his jumpsuit-and-lifts wearing "friend" was innocent of harboring nuclear ambitions and, further, swear he would shave his famous moustache if proved wrong. Days later there would be a missile strike on South Korea, you would be a prisoner of war, and Geraldo would finally shave off that moustache. In prison.

Or trapped among the Donners with Joan?

As Joan says, even cannibals dress to impress. So why not try to sell them jewelry, clothing, and perfume? Freezing temperatures and lack of nutrition can play havoc with skin tone, too, so a little Rivers-branded face cream might also be in order. Though forced to bring her along, if you're lucky she won't invite Melissa.

The Donners began their ill-fated journey from Illinois to California early in 1846 but in July broke from the main group of emigrants heading west, in search of a shortcut between the Rockies and the Sierra Nevada mountains. Instead of reaching the mountain pass in August or early September as planned, they instead fell behind schedule and arrived in late October to a fierce snowstorm, the beginning of the worst winter in Sierra history. While there's no official record of what caused the Donners to be late, it's probable that Joan pestered each member for a pointless, extended interview on the "hay carpet" to discuss the latest in settler fashion: "Who are you wearing? Levi Strauss? *Fabulous!*"

Once stranded and cut off by snow from resupply, you and the Donners would initially resort to slaughtering work animals and boiling shoe leather for sustenance. Joan's catty comments about the Donners needing to "skip a meal anyway" would certainly not win you any friends among the family members. A fervent animal rights activist and vegetarian, Joan would probably suggest cooking up some seitan steaks or tempeh and beans, not particularly helpful recommendations considering the circumstances.

Joan's harsh brand of humor would probably not go over well with the starving Donners. Throwaway lines like, "I wouldn't touch that cellulite with a ten-foot fork!" and "Honey, the only meat on you is sitting on your neck!" might create some discord, as would the fact that, at 90 percent plastic, Joan herself would be inedible.

But the worst part of the trip would clearly be the incessant sales pitching. Bad snowstorms make for captive audiences, and Joan knows when an audience is hungry—to buy. You and the Donners will sit around the cabin, eyes glazed, tongues swollen, as you hear all about Joan Rivers Beauty, a continually expanding line that encompasses her uniquely formulated Joan Rivers Results skin care products, color cosmetics, and luxury fragrances: Now & Forever and the new, captivating Pink Flowers eau de parfum. Beginning her pitch with the federally trademarked "Can we talk?", Joan will describe limited-time offers of "cannibal cream" and "rigor moisturizer" aimed at her target market. The most disturbing aspect of the whole trip will be watching the Donners age before your eyes while Joan just looks younger and younger. What's her secret?

North Korea or Donner Pass? Gerald Michael Rivera or Joan Sandra Molinsky? Two highly paid stars with a love of the lime-light and a nose (broken or sculpted) for viewers. Either way, it's showtime!

Things can't get much worse than being anywhere near the eruption of Krakatoa, the most destructive volcano in recorded history. Throw in Gopher, Julie McCoy, Doc, and Captain Stubing and you've got the makings of a course for misadventure. But wait. Is that Old Blue Eyes himself, scotch rocks in one hand and you chained to the other, preparing to run with the bulls? Things just got worse. This is going to be some vacation.

A cruise to Krakatoa . . .

The loudest sound ever historically reported isn't the conga line on the Lido deck, it's the eruption of Krakatoa, which blew apart massively and with disastrous global consequences on August

26–27, 1883. It sent shock waves around the world, killed thirty thousand, and generated waves one hundred feet high. You remembered your sea sickness pills, right?

Obviously, Captain Stubing has been too busy chatting up the divorcees to read his marine forecasts, otherwise he'd be well aware that in the years preceding the eruption the volcano was generating enormous earthquakes, some felt thousands of miles away. In May of 1883, steam began venting from Krakatoa, and in early August plumes of ash began shooting into the sky. Nevertheless, the *Pacific Princess* set out for Indonesia seemingly ready for any eventuality—as long as it could be handled by Doc and his medical bag.

You will be forgiven for being entranced by the terrific dancing troupe known as the "Love Boat Mermaids" (wait, isn't that Teri Hatcher?) and ignoring the danger signs: the large pumice stones bouncing into the Crystal Pool, the steeply sloped Captain's Table, the ash falling into your piña colada (just ask Isaac for an umbrella). You learn that Gopher can't get a date, "Ace" Covington is accidentally dating a mother and her daughter at the same time, and Vicki is still a whiny brat, and you assume that all is right with the world. But when Julie begins organizing "hot lava night," and the laugh track begins to melt, you suspect that you're approaching not Acapulco or Mazatlan but the Sunda Strait and Krakatoa.

Your worst fears are likely to be confirmed as you see superheated gasses speeding away from Krakatoa, actually causing the pyroclastic flows to "float" on the ocean water, suspended on beds of hot steam. The fiery magma entering the ocean surrounding the volcano displaces many cubic miles of water, causing huge waves to swamp the *Princess* and almost knocking off Charo's top.

In an instant, the Aloha, Lido, Fiesta, Promenade, and Riviera decks are underwater, the *Princess* is listing badly, and someone has stolen Betty White's diamond brooch! No, wait, it was there in her cabin the whole time. Whew.

The weight off all that water and ash, combined with all the guest stars, is going to sink the ship—and you with it. The volcano's ejected dust particles will circle the globe and cool the atmosphere for years after the eruption, causing cold temperatures and spectacular sunsets. But from its watery grave the Love Boat will rise and set sail again, this time as *Love Boat: The Next Wave*. At least you won't be alive to watch it.

▬▬ Or the running of the bulls with Frank? ▬▬

There's little doubt that, when it comes to running with the bulls—or doing pretty much anything with the Chairman of the Board—Frank's in charge. Unfortunately, with your hand cuffed to his, you're together, and you'll never walk alone. When the bulls come charging through the streets of Pamplona, well, life's a trippy thing, and anything goes.

On a foggy day, in stormy weather, the angry beasts will be released in the wee small hours of the morning and you and Frank, like the other fools, rush in. To make your escape easier, you might consider asking Frank, "Can't we be friends while we're swingin' down the lane?" His likely reply, "I've heard that song before," will amply demonstrate that it's all about Frank, and that you're nothing but a man alone. Then, a little too close for comfort, he'll demand, "Why should I cry over you?" "Look to your heart," you might reply. "Please be kind!" His reply, "I don't stand a ghost of a chance with you. Anytime, anywhere!" His brusque intonation that "I get along without you very well" will end the discussion.

You will hear the hooves pounding the pavement as the bulls begin their charge toward you. You begin racing down the streets of Pamplona with Frank taunting the bulls, yelling wildly, "I get a kick out of you!" At this point, you might tell Frank, "It worries me, let's get away from it all!" Consider suggesting other places to travel, perhaps leaving on a jet plane for Brazil, Chicago, the Isle of Capri, London by night, April in Paris, autumn in New York, or south of the border. While trying to avoid being gored, Frank will probably tell you that you've got nothing in common, except that "I'm walking behind you." Trying to take it nice and easy, with only five minutes more, you have high hopes that you'll make it all the way.

Then, suddenly, taking a long drag on his cigarette and a swig of scotch, the Chairman turns to face you. "Ya better stop," he says. "It's nice to go trav'ling. But it's a lonesome road, and the nearness of you . . . well, I'm a man alone. It's over, it's over, it's over!" At this point, desperation is likely to set in. "But, Frank," you'll plead, "I'm not afraid. Just try a little tenderness! Talk to me! I'm close to you, Frank. Call me irresponsible! Blame it on my youth. But I've had my moments, and it all depends on you. We're chained together, and I'm a fool to want you, but when the world was young, well, no one ever tells you . . ." You'll continue with a final plea: "Frank, you do something to me! You'd be so nice to come home to. I'll never be the same! I'll never smile again!"

"Kid," Frank will say with surprising tenderness, "I can't believe you're in love with me. We're just friends. Don't worry about me; we'll be together again. I don't like good-byes. But some-where along the way, as time goes by, in all my tomorrows, I'll see you again." Producing a key to the handcuffs, Frank will unlock you and turn to walk away, leaving you to fend for yourself. "Kid, don'cha go 'way mad," he'll say. "This isn't my kind of town, and, softly, as I leave you tonight, put your dreams away (for another day). I thought about you, and I believe I'm gonna love you, and it worries me. But then, I'm drinking again. I'll be around, though. Maybe you'll be there. And I'll see you again, and not as a stranger. So long, kid, I'll be seeing you. Sleep warm."

As you face the charging bulls alone, you'll realize the hurt doesn't go away. Here's to the losers, you'll say to yourself, but dry your eyes. The saddest thing of all is a secret love, and somewhere in your heart, you'll know you'll never walk alone. You and Frank will always be together.

Then you'll be trampled to death.

Set a course for adventure . . . But will it be toward an erupting volcano or fleeing from angry bulls attached to Frank? Pumice on the poop deck or the Chairman chafing your wrist? The erup-tion of Krakatoa killed tens of thousands. A stampede of bulls could maim or kill you in seconds. But what if *Frank* got hurt? Then you'd *really* be in trouble.

She's the empress of entertaining, the doyenne of dining, the queen of the green thumb. Or at least her staff is. She's Martha, Inc., and she's going to help you transform the Taliban's dusty mountain redoubt into a sunny place you'll be happy to call a hideout. They are two rich, loudmouthed radio talk show hosts, sworn enemies who never met a stripper or a prescription they didn't like. They are Howard and Rush. They've both clawed their way back to the top, and now they're in your backseat, enabling you to use the carpool lane. But, alas, traffic is at a standstill. Which will it be, Tora Bora or the 10 freeway?

If anyone can, Martha will certainly whip the Taliban's winter "escape" into shape. But before you can even consider redecorating, you'll have to take stock (though not ImClone stock) of the caves, and perhaps do a little spring cleaning.

Step one is a complete inventory of the entire Tora Bora cave complex. First, find a dry-erase board and markers—use sand and a stick if a dry-erase board isn't available—and organize the complex into rooms: kitchen, living and dining, barracks, radio room, ammo dump, and so on. If you think of it, consider taking digital photos of each room—or even painting each room in watercolors!—and posting them under their proper headings. Make a list of every item in every room. Using scissors, a pen, a ruler, and construction paper (for best results, use sixty-five-pound test), make cutouts to represent each item in each room. For example, cut out tiny AK-47s to represent rifles; small apple-shaped pieces for grenades (don't forget the stem, that's the pin!); and long, curvy, snakelike pieces for the ammo belts. Using double-sided tape, move the items from room to room on the board until you're happy with how things are arranged. Then redecorate the entire complex. Don't forget: guests will typically gather in the room with the fire pit, so make sure there's plenty of ground seating (boulders, tree stumps) for everyone to be comfortable. Consider placing the satellite radio in this room to add some background music. Keep the volume low so your guests can chat, and also to prevent the Special Forces from pinpointing your location.

Martha *loves* cooking for a caveful of people, and she will probably instruct you first to go out into the garden and snip some flowers and herbs to garnish the serving platters. Fortunately, Afghanistan is known for its sunny, dry growing season and you should find an abundant crop of poppies nearby. Even if you're on good terms with them, however, remember to check with the neighboring warlords before venturing onto their property for poppy picking. (And watch for booby traps!) You might even consider inviting them to the cave complex for dinner; this will head off any possible complaints about noise and gunshots later on.

Just before setting the table, sweep out the entire cave complex and empty the latrines; place small bunches of lavender, tied together with purple ribbon, next to the waste buckets. Put a fresh coat of whitewash on the walls and place a pot of mulled cider on the fire—the coals should be ash-covered, not glowing orange—to give the place a warm, welcoming scent. Place a party favor at each setting (three rocket-propelled grenades tied together with daisies are always appreciated; fresh clips of ammo painted in cheery colors will have everyone talking) so the guests will have something to take home after dinner. Greet each guest at the cave entrance with a mug of your "battle brew," your own homemade beer (don't neglect to make a batch of nonalcoholic) and give each freedom fighter a hand-knitted name tag. The laser-guided bombs and "daisy cutters" dropping on the complex are your signal to marshal everyone to the table. Finally, when everyone is seated and the hurricane lamps are lighted, Martha will instruct you to bring out the meal.

This may very well be the best Yankee pot roast you've ever tasted. *Bon appétit!*

They always claim that if you don't like what they're saying, you can change the station. But what if, for once, that's not an option? It's the office carpool from hell, with Howard and Rush sharing the backseat and the soapbox. Forget arguing over the armrest, these two blowhards may actually come to blows. And a game of "I spy" probably isn't going to distract them.

The bad news is that Howard is no longer constrained by the FCC, so he's not likely to pull any punches when it comes to giving you backseat driving advice. "Hey $%&#@, I told you to take surface streets, you $#%&ing @!%*#er," he might begin. "Don't you know that the King of All Media can't be *#$%ing late?" Meanwhile, Rush will instruct you to "keep moving right" and explain that the carpool lane is on the left due to a liberal bias in the Department of Transportation. He will go on to pillory you for driving a "foreign" car (even though it's made in the USA by American workers) and warn you not to get in an accident, lest you hit an "illegal" without insurance. In fact, Rush will point out that all the traffic is actually being caused by the "freeloaders" who snuck in across the border and are now driving cars instead of looking for work in Mexico.

Howard will point out his disappointment with the fact that the "median strip" is actually not a dance club for scantily clad women but a barrier between traffic lanes. Noticing the traffic moving well in the other direction, he will probably inquire if you'd be willing to "go both ways" and, if so, can he watch? Soon he'll complain that he "has to take a leak" while casually mentioning that he had "a rest stop in New Jersey" named after him.

Not to be outdone, Rush will accuse Howard of being in the "cut-and-run crowd," unwilling and afraid to "stay the course" and pee his pants. Then he'll light a fat cigar.

With the car inching forward, you will begin to feel nausea creeping over you. As you open the window to throw up, Rush will accuse you of being a "weak-kneed liberal" and leading "the war on manliness." Howard will pull out a pill bottle filled with prescription drugs and ask Rush if he "needs a refill." As the two men begin trading insults and throwing punches in the back seat, you turn on the radio in a desperate search for Al Franken. But he's no longer on Air America. You put on NPR but it's the monthly beg-a-thon. Then you get a piece of luck: it's Pat Robertson and the 700 Club. You're saved! Praise the Lord!

Tora Bora or traffic? Martha, or Howard and the "ditto head"? Hey, things could always be worse. You could be their personal assistant.

WHICH WOULD BE WORSE, INITIATION NIGHT AT THE HELLS ANGELS BOOK CLUB OR FLIGHT TRAINING AT KAMIKAZE PILOT SCHOOL?

Joining a book club (or a sewing circle) always held great appeal for you, but learning to fly is your real dream. But what if you had to choose one or the other? And what if each activity was made a bit more, um, challenging through the addition of a group of burly bikers and the fact that the only flight school with an opening is for kamikaze pilots? Things could become dangerous in a hurry if you haven't read this week's book—or the flight plan.

=== **Hells Angels book club . . .** ===

They're big, loud, and intimidating. They smell of grease and motor oil, and they're usually splattered with dead bugs. You often see them in large groups congregated around bars. And when you hear them coming, you'd best get out of their way. Yes, Harley-Davidson motorcycles are a sure sign that their owners, members of the Hells Angels Motorcycle Club (HAMC), are nearby. And it looks as though they're carrying this month's book: it's initiation night. You did do the reading, right?

The Hells Angels Motorcycle Club was founded in Fontana, California, just after World War II and is considered the father of all motorcycle clubs in the nation. The use of the name "Hells Angels" by the HAMC is attributed to various sources (including the 1930 Howard Hughes film *Hell's Angels*) but, according to the club itself, it most likely comes from a suggestion by Arvid Olsen, who was an associate of the club's founding members and the squadron leader of the 3rd Pursuit Squadron "Hell's Angels" American Volunteer Group during the war. In sheer numbers, the HAMC has fallen behind many of its rivals, including the Outlaws, Mongols, and Misfits (no record on their book-of-the-month selections). But the Angel's outsized history of ferocity and lawlessness—as well as the rogues gallery of its members currently serving long prison sentences—has permanently cemented the Angels' reputation as the prototypical biker gang. But what might initiation night look like when they open the books for you . . . and then begin peppering you with questions about plot structure, character development, and story arc?

A deadbolt is thrown back, a heavy iron door swings inward, and you peer anxiously into a dark, low-ceilinged room. A hulking giant of a man, with a head like a cinderblock and hands that could tear a phone book in half, stands behind the door and grunts a gruff welcome. Stepping inside, your eyes begin to adjust to the gloom as you notice a bar, cheap wood paneling, beer mirrors, and a badly stained pool table. A veil of cigarette smoke hangs over your face as you just make out a well-stocked bookshelf full of leather-bound volumes leaning crazily against one wall, weighted down by first editions. A small clutch of very big men in boots sit silently in a circle, facing you. There's one empty seat. It's a rocking chair with a small quilted pillow on the seat. It must be yours. A confusing odor, at once frightening and comforting. After a few seconds you can place it: it's the scent of sweat, leather, Jack Daniel's, and chamomile tea. . . .

The peak and the valley of the HAMC came at the same moment, the infamous incident at Altamont Speedway on December 6, 1969—an event later documented in the 1970 film *Gimme Shelter*. Gang members had been hired to protect the stage and provide security (allegedly in exchange for several dozen cases of beer), but when several members' motorcycles were damaged by the crowd a melee ensued, and a concertgoer was stabbed to death. Much of the club's negative image can be attributed to this incident, but a groundbreaking 1965 article by Hunter S. Thompson called "The Motorcycle Gangs" also helped to establish the view among law enforcement agencies (and the general public) that club members were violent good-for-nothings bent on mayhem. A string of federal prosecutions beginning in the 1970s, mostly for drugs and violent crimes, sent many leaders to prison, and violence between the Angels and other biker gangs also culled the ranks. Certainly, numbers have dwindled over the years, and club leaders typically blame any illegalities on rogue members acting alone and without club sanction. Similarly, though the Angels have steadfastly denied involvement in any sort of reading circle, coffee klatch, or book club, it's been said that a special patch—an image of Moby-Dick with a dagger through it—denotes membership in this dangerous and well-read group.

> *Initiation into the exclusive inner reading circle of the Angels is fraught with danger. You're required to quote, verbatim, from* Pilgrim's Progress, Siddhartha, *and* Zen and the Art of Motorcycle Maintenance. *Even the slightest mistake results in a severe reprimand or a punch from a fist wrapped in a tea cozy. In addition, members of the HABC wear a length of hand-knitted wool scarf around their necks, which can be pulled off in an instant and used as a garrote.*
>
> *Though details of the initiation rights are secret, you hear rumors that that each green recruit (known as an "uncracked spine") must offer all existing members (known as "dog ears") complimentary use of his bookmark, highlighting pen, and Itty Bitty Book Light. Members may take turns with these items and then pass them around for other dog ears to use and abuse for as long as they like. The use of "study aids" such as NoDoz and Mountain Dew is also said to be widespread.*
>
> *Should you survive initiation night, you'll probably be sprayed with beer and given a personalized, patch-covered coat (the notorious "dust jacket") to wear with pride. Should you fail the test, well, you'll be "remaindered."*

Or kamikaze flight school?

You've always dreamed of learning how to pilot a small plane. Well, get ready for a special, one-time-only offer of flying lessons in your very own, purpose-built aircraft designed for speed—but not for landing. You'll be joined by a number of other young, idealistic pilots seeking more glory than experience, a group nicknamed "the crash test dummies."

Near the end of World War II, as the Japanese Pacific fleet began suffering increasing losses to U.S. naval and air attacks, the Japanese hold on the strategically critical Philippines began to loosen. The commandant of Japan's 1st Air Fleet, Vice Admiral Takijiro Onishi, decided to form a *shinpū tokubetsu kōgeki tai*, or "divine wind special attack unit." The admiral understood that newer American planes, particularly the Corsair and Hellcat, were faster and more maneuverable than Japan's aging aircraft, and that only attacks on American aircraft carrier battle groups were likely to slow the Allied advance.

Onishi asked Commander Asaiki Tamai to assemble an all-volunteer group of skilled airmen to pilot the suicide planes, which would be stripped down and loaded with explosives. On October 25–26, 1944, fifty-five kamikaze from the special attack unit plowed into the HMAS *Australia*, USS *Sangamon*, USS *Suwannee*, USS *Santee*, and a number of escort vessels. A total of seven aircraft carriers were hit, and by the end of the day on the twenty-sixth, forty ships were damaged or sunk. It didn't help that most U.S. aircraft carriers has wooden flight decks.

As a new pilot showing up at the airfield for your lesson, you may be greeted by your flight instructor with "*Irashaimasu!*" which, loosely translated, means "don't bother putting on your seatbelt." Sensing your confusion, the flight instructor may laugh at his joke and assure you that he is just kidding, that in fact you will be securely harnessed into the pilot's seat (so securely, in fact, that you will not be able to parachute out).

You will meet the other members of your flight class. To a man, the pilots are likely to be intensely focused individuals particularly uninterested in getting to know you in any way. A suggestion that you meet later for beers will probably be greeted with blank stares. You might consider flipping through the kamikaze pilot's manual to learn more about your training. Oddly, the manual will probably have very little practical flying advice. And, in fact, there's no section on landing at all.

Transcend life and death. When you eliminate all thoughts about life and death, you will be able to totally disregard your earthly life. This will also enable you to concentrate your attention on eradicating the enemy with unwavering determination, meanwhile reinforcing your excellence in flight skills.

The flowing, almost poetic language is a nice change from the dry text usually found in such books, but the part about eliminating thoughts of life and death is rather ominous.

Out on the tarmac, you and your fellow kamikazes will inspect the planes, Nakajima Ki-115 *Tsurugi*. The aircraft will probably appear extremely light—most likely because the fuselages are made of canvas and wood. Not exactly sturdy or safe. Climbing up a ladder, you might peek into the cockpit. The controls will be rudimentary and, oddly, the ejection mechanism may be missing. Climbing down, you may notice the landing gear is of the "breakaway" variety and is to be jettisoned just after takeoff. You point out that this could make for a bumpy and dangerous landing. This will certainly be greeted with more stares and snickers.

 **CHOICE BITS**

* Members of the Hells Angels must ride Harley-Davidson motorcycles.

* Loosely translated, *kamikaze* means "divine wind" and refers to a mythic typhoon that is said to have swamped Mongol invaders attacking Japan in the thirteenth century.

* Seventy U.S. Navy vessels were reportedly damaged or destroyed by kamikaze pilots.

Most kamikaze pilots were very young, typically no older than twenty-two, and sometimes as young as sixteen; about four thousand lost their lives. According to the U.S. Navy, about 2,800 kamikaze attackers sunk 34 Navy ships, damaged 368 others, killed 4,900 sailors, and wounded over 4,800. Fourteen percent of kamikazes survived massive barrages of antiaircraft fire to score a hit on a ship. Maybe you'll be one of the lucky few!

Outlaw book club or kamikaze flight of fancy? The Hells Angels aren't exactly known for their welcoming embrace of strangers—and your Japanese motorcycle may not win you many Brownie points. On the other hand, the life expectancy for kamikaze pilots falls neatly into the "one and done" category.

Choosing the right wine for a get-together can be *so* frustrating. Red or white? Champagne or *Prosecco*? Bottle or box? That's why society types leave the job to the professionals and hire a party planner. The expert selects several vintages for you to sample, and also helps you organize and plan the whole shindig. But what happens when the whole party-planning process becomes a battle, literally? What to do when you're faced with sampling wines while wearing a gas mask and avoiding enemy machine gun fire? Or when your party planner has a résumé that's somewhat suspect—particularly the list of successful events? It's time to lock and load, dig in, and keep a good head on your shoulders.

As a general point, life in a World War I battlefield trench or dug-out is not likely to be particularly conducive to sampling wine. Holding a glass above the parapet and up to the light to view color and clarity is likely to result in a burst of machine gun fire or a shot from a sniper's rifle. For similar reasons, you should also avoid the urge to peek out of the trench. While tasting, you should be seated comfortably but, to prevent choking, not reclining. Crouching low is acceptable.

In the trenches, the wine must be stored on its side to prevent the cork from drying out. Place bottles between sandbags to prevent them from slipping and breaking. Of course, bullets of any caliber are the scourge of wine bottles everywhere, and smaller targets are the order of the day in the trenches. Thus, be sure the narrow necks of the bottles, not the wider bottoms, face the enemy. Cold nights huddled in the mud may be uncomfortable for you, but cool temperatures are always friendly to wine, provided there is no freeze. Wine will warm (or cool) to the ambient temperature at a rate of about 4 degrees per ten minutes of exposure. However, white phosphorus artillery shells are incendiary weapons and their use by the enemy may result in intense heat that can spoil even the most carefully stored vintages. Should your fellow trenchmates yell "Incoming!", immediately throw your body on top of the bottles to protect them.

Older vintages of red wine will benefit from decanting, because this allows more of the wine's surface area to react with oxygen, and serves to separate the sediment (which may cause a bitter taste) from the wine itself. The decanter should be made of glass and be very clean—but never use harsh, abrasive chemicals to remove impurities! Keep the bottle angled as you pour the wine to prevent the sediment from exiting the bottle and entering the decanter. Twist the bottle as you raise it to prevent drips. If you cannot locate a decanter, use your helmet.

Finding intact crystal stemware in a trench is likely to be a major challenge. In a pinch, you may sip the wine from a tin cup or a canteen, but be aware that this may result in an off or metallic taste. Between shellings and patrols into no-man's-land, sit back and savor the wine. Take a good-sized sip and move the wine around on your tongue so that all your taste buds come into contact with it. In the muck, you may discover that older vintages have an earthy, smoky, flinty flavor, with hints of ersatz coffee and cigarettes and an undercurrent of stale biscuit. When sampling a good wine, take note of the "nose," or overall smell of the wine. "Trench" wine may carry an aroma of latrine, mustard gas, and rotting corpse. Remember not to swallow the wine but to carefully spit it out into a container, lest you get drunk, fall asleep, and be overrun. Wines from Germany are likely to be strong, seductive, robust, and potent, but ultimately empty. American wines will be heady, assertive, full-bodied, and full of character and grit. French wines will be soft, delicate, and graceful, but with a tendency to fade before the finish. Swiss wines will be neutral.

=========== **Or party planning with Custer?** ===========

Things are likely to get off to a rocky start when Custer—blond mane a-flowing and big moustache a-drooping—immediately dismisses your desire for careful planning and instead recommends a "raiding party." Confused as to what the ultimate price of such a function might be, you begin asking about cost. Barreling through your backyard on his steed, Custer ignores your queries, unsheathes his cutlass, and yells, "Forget the cash! *Let's charge!*"

You should consider calling for references before committing to Custer Strategic Event Planning. You might discover that he graduated dead last in his class at West Point, receiving a failing grade for his thesis "French War–Fighting Techniques: An Effective Deterrent to Future German Aggression." Several days after graduation, as officer of the guard Custer failed to stop a fight between two cadets and was court-martialed; he narrowly escaped punishment due to the outbreak of the Civil War.

Before going into party planning, Custer led several cavalry units during the war, almost all of which had very high casualty rates (even by the standards of the day). Nevertheless, after the South's surrender Custer's never-say-die attitude and military connections got him a posting as lieutenant colonel of the 7th Cavalry regiment, an outfit tasked with running the Cheyenne off their land. In 1867 Custer was again court-martialed and suspended from duty for being absent from duty during the campaign. He claimed it was all a mixup having to do with an apparently mangled message from headquarters that he understood to read "take a break" when it actually said "you may be court-marshaled for dereliction of duty." Custer was later removed from his command by President Ulysses S. Grant before being reinstated due to public pressure.

Your careful plan for the event includes waiting for all guests to arrive and begin mingling in the backyard, enjoying cocktails before the food service begins. You specifically order Custer to linger in the kitchen with his men and await your command to start. The headstrong Custer, however, has little respect for the capabilities of "firewater drinkers and savages" and believes he can surprise the guests and staff with a sudden, overwhelming surge. Ignoring your orders for a laid-back, leisurely paced celebration, he will command his small squad of mounted servers to charge into the room, carving knives drawn. Unbeknownst to Custer, however, many invitees have brought friends and the ranks of the guests have swelled—and most are well-armed with drink swords and flaming kebobs.

Following standard cavalry and party-helper doctrine, Custer will first order his men to the high ground and then to dismount. He will then command one out of every five men to corral five now riderless horses—effectively reducing his attacking force by 20 percent. From this point on, your gathering will degenerate

 **CHOICE BITS**

* "Trench foot" was a fungal infection that resulted from wet trench grime entering abrasions in the foot. To combat it, soldiers were ordered to change socks twice a day.

* An unofficial "breakfast truce" was observed in the mornings by both sides during trench warfare, allowing soldiers to eat.

* Every soldier in Custer's detachment was killed at Little Bighorn. The only survivor was a horse named, oddly enough, Comanche.

* Custer was not scalped, though many of his men were.

into a violent and vicious food fight, with the vastly outnumbered Custer and his troops attempting to make a final stand behind the dessert table. This so-called Battle of *Petit Fours* (Battle of Little Snack Cakes) will go down in history as one of the worst massacres in military and event-planner history.

Wine tasting in the trenches or Custer's cavaliers in your backyard? Either way, when the smoke clears you'll be knee-deep in broken glass.

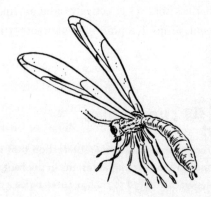

WHICH WOULD BE WORSE, TEN HOURS IN BAGHDAD OR TEN HOURS IN BALTIMORE?

Someone once said that Beirut is (or used to be) the Paris of the Middle East. That may be true. But Baghdad is the Baltimore of Iraq, and neither city has ever been mistaken for Paris. Take a stroll in the well-fortified "Green Zone" or the heavily patrolled inner harbor. But wander just beyond their boundaries and you'll face the modern urban crime environment, with corruption, assault, murder, and mayhem—and official crime statistics that no one quite believes. Pack your bags—and your sidearm—for a night on the town you'll never forget. Assuming you make it home.

Your visit will begin with an exciting, high-velocity ride on the "Highway of Death," the scenic stretch of interstate that runs from the airport to the city center. Skip a regular taxi in favor of an "up-armored" Humvee with a machine gun and Marine escort. Make certain your seat belt is fastened and your body armor is in place.

Upon arrival downtown, you'll almost certainly face language barriers. However, the concrete blast barriers are likely to be a larger inconvenience as you try to see the sites—at least the ones that haven't been blown up yet. Baghdad is the cradle of civilization, so don't miss a visit to the National Museum of Iraq. Sadly, the museum's once-impressive collection of antiquities has shrunk markedly since March of 2003, and most treasures are now in "private collections." But, as one official noted at the time, "stuff happens."

If your rental car doesn't come with a full tank, much of your ten hours in Baghdad is likely to be spent in an endless gasoline line—though regular electricity shortages may mean the pumps aren't working anyway. The good news is that gas is about sixty cents a gallon. The bad news is that troublemakers tend to blow up the pipelines on a regular basis. Consider seeing downtown by up-armored bicycle.

Like any big city, Baghdad has some areas that are best avoided after dark (though regular dusk-to-dawn curfews may keep you off the streets anyway). In particular, 100 percent of the downtown area beyond the blast-fortified walls of the Green Zone should be considered off-limits. It should be noted that the Green (or "Occupied") Zone is relatively safe most of the time. However, the shrill "whistling" sounds that can occasionally be heard are not doormen trying to summon cabs but rather incoming mortar rounds. Drop your camera and leap into the nearest foxhole or sandbagged fortification during these times. Also, avoid hanging around checkpoints and markets, and mingling in crowds of police recruits.

A word about crime. Baghdad's official city motto ("It just *looks* like civil war!") could just as easily be replaced by the unofficial one: "Every month, a new murder record!" Death never takes a holiday in Baghdad and, unfortunately, there is no prime "killing season" that can be avoided. On a typical day, a dozen bullet-riddled bodies are found in the capital, car bombs or roadside bombs kill a dozen more, and several people are kidnapped. The busiest building in Baghdad is the city morgue, which typically sees about 1,500 bodies per month—and those are just the ones they know about. One estimate has put the death toll in Iraq since March 2003 at six hundred thousand, or about fifteen thousand killings per month.

Should you fall victim to crime, it's typically best to avoid filing a report with the local police (sometimes referred to by the locals as "death squads"). To further confuse things, the criminal element in Baghdad may be wearing police uniforms, or the police may be covering up their crimes, or the police officers themselves may be the criminals committing the crimes—no one is quite sure. In any case, if you do make it ten hours without encountering any violence be sure to alert someone in the U.S. military's press office. They're always looking for good news.

Baltimore, Maryland (sometimes pronounced "Bodymore, Murderland"), is Baghdad-on-the-Atlantic. Day after day, week after week, the bodies pile up, and robberies, rapes, assaults, and thefts trounce national averages. Venture out beyond the relative safety of the Inner Harbor and Camden Yards and, as in Iraq, you'll find a virtual civil war—except that in Baltimore, U.S. taxpayers aren't pouring in $195 million per day trying to stop it.

A perennial contender for America's most dangerous big city, Baltimore even beats out Detroit in most crime categories. These include murder (43.5 per 100,000 people versus 42.1 for Detroit, versus 5.5 for the national average); robbery (638.5 per 100,000 versus 596.2 for Detroit, versus 136.7 for the national average); and aggravated assault (1,128.7 per 100,000 versus 1,023.5 for Detroit, versus 291.1 for the national average). In 1999, Baltimore mayor Martin O'Malley promised to get the city's murder rate down to 175. By 2005 it was 269. And it's still climbing. The city now averages about five murders per week.

For your ten hours in Baltimore you should plan the timing of your trip carefully. The weather can be cold during the winter months, with a frigid wind blowing in from the east. But a drippy nose may be the least of your problems in January, Baltimore's deadliest month. There were thirty-three murders in January, 2005; one cold January day featured five homicides. Even if you get a good deal on a hotel, Wednesdays and Saturdays should also be avoided as these tend to be the deadliest days of the week; during the rest of the week, the homicides are pretty evenly distributed.

Iraq may be awash in guns—each Baghdad family is allowed one, but *only* one, AK-47 assault rifle—but Baltimoreans, too, like their firearms, and there seems to be a "no limit" rule to the number one can possess. In the first six months of 2006, federal prosecutors indicted sixty-five gun felony cases, a 50 percent increase over 2005. But that's only half the story. City prosecutors actually lost more gun cases at trial in 2005 than they won. Remember, this is the city where the TV show *Homicide: Life on the Streets* was set. Baltimore has had seven police commissioners in seven years.

Thinking about doing some shopping during your visit? You may want to think again. A recent survey placed Baltimore dead last (twenty-fifth out of twenty-five cities surveyed) in customer service. In Baltimore, people waiting in line—at the grocery store, at the bank, while shopping, even at fast food joints—have to wait an average of five minutes and thirteen seconds to get service. Perhaps you're thinking about having a nice dinner out? It will be a leisurely meal, because Baltimore also ranks last in the amount of time diners have to wait to have their orders taken—even at the best restaurants in town.

On the bright side, the Baltimore Aquarium is quite nice, and the hard shell crabs are delicious. And, should you decide to make Baltimore your home, your children should have a relatively easy time of it in school. In 2006, the passing grade in Baltimore city schools was lowered from 70 to 60. Hey, six out of ten ain't bad!

Which murderous metropolis will it be? Baghdad's got the sun, while Baltimore's got the sea. In one sense, it really doesn't matter which city you choose. Because if you can make it there, you'll make it anywhere.

APPENDIX

Compare with friends, argue with enemies:

☐ Genghis Khan	*or*	☐ Attila the Hun
☐ Mao	*or*	☑ McCarthy
☐ Napoleon	*or*	☑ Nixon
☑ Hitler	*or*	☐ Hussein
☐ Lorena	*or*	☐ Lizzie
☐ Manson	*or*	☐ Dahmer
☐ Ozzy	*or*	☑ Marilyn
☑ Manilow	*or*	☐ Diamond
☐ Flesh-eating bacteria	*or*	☑ Leprosy
☐ Poison ivy	*or*	☐ Mistletoe
☐ Black plague	*or*	☑ Spanish flu
☐ Smallpox	*or*	☑ Small handgun
☐ Boil	*or*	☐ Goiter
☑ Pyramids	*or*	☐ Panama Canal
☐ Ebola	*or*	☑ Asbestos
☑ Appendicitis	*or*	☐ Audit
☐ Gladiator	*or*	☑ Grave robber
☐ T. rex	*or*	☐ Tyson
☐ Werewolf	*or*	☑ Dracula
☐ Tony Soprano	*or*	☐ Tony Montana
☐ Terminator	*or*	☑ Hal 9000
☑ Darth Vader	*or*	☐ Don Corleone
☐ Alien	*or*	☑ Predator
☐ Cheney	*or*	☐ Bin Laden
☐ Neanderthals	*or*	☐ Ninjas
☐ West Nile mosquito	*or*	☐ West African dictator
☐ Black widow	*or*	☐ Giant centipede
☐ Barracuda	*or*	☐ Man-of-war
☐ Pack of wolves	*or*	☐ Pack of cigarettes
☐ Rats	*or*	☐ Rambo
☐ Vampire bats	*or*	☐ Hookworms
☐ Jaws	*or*	☐ Godzilla
☐ Harvester ants	*or*	☐ Rattlesnakes
☐ Chopping onions	*or*	☐ Making sausage
☐ Neverland Ranch	*or*	☐ Poultry-processing plant
☐ Geraldo	*or*	☐ Joan
☐ Love Boat to Krakatoa	*or*	☐ Bulls with Frank Sinatra
☐ Tora Bora with Martha	*or*	☐ Traffic with Howard and Rush
☐ Hells Angels book club	*or*	☐ Kamikaze pilot school
☐ Wine tasting in the trenches	*or*	☐ Party planning with Custer
☐ Baghdad	*or*	☐ Baltimore

BAD VS. WORSE ALTERNATE MATCHUPS

Prompt	Option A	or	Option B
Barber?	☐ Ozzy	or	☐ Bin Laden
Football coach?	☐ Tony Soprano	or	☐ Tyson
Caterer?	☐ Alien	or	☐ Cheney
In an alley?	☐ Rats	or	☐ Dracula
Steak dinner?	☐ Neanderthals	or	☐ Lorena
House pet?	☐ Black widow	or	☐ Nixon
Once per week?	☐ Goiter	or	☐ Poison ivy
Visiting North Korea with?	☐ Manilow	or	☐ Terminator
Marry your daughter off to?	☐ Darth Vader	or	☐ Tony Montana
Perform at the bar mitzvah?	☐ Rambo	or	☐ Don Corleone
Release accidentally?	☐ Jaws	or	☐ Ninjas
Camp counselor?	☐ Joan	or	☐ Predator
Wake up to?	☐ Giant centipede	or	☐ Appendicitis
Breakfast cereal?	☐ Sausage	or	☐ Onions
Caterer?	☐ Werewolf	or	☐ West African dictator
In your salad?	☐ Hookworms	or	☐ Rattlesnakes
Fifteen-hour road trip with?	☐ Vampire bats	or	☐ Pack of wolves
Running the blood drive?	☐ T. rex	or	☐ West Nile mosquito
Notice in your housing development?	☐ Poultry-processing plant	or	☐ Tora Bora
IT guy?	☐ Predator	or	☐ Geraldo
Ten hours in?	☐ Neverland Ranch	or	☐ The trenches
Father?	☐ Howard Stern	or	☐ Rush Limbaugh
Science teacher?	☐ Frank Sinatra	or	☐ Custer
General contractor?	☐ Martha	or	☐ Hells Angels
In your slipper?	☐ Man-of-War	or	☐ Harvester ants

Share a cubicle with?	☐ The cast of *Jackass*	*or*	☐ _____
Interview your daughter for a job?	☐ Hugh Hefner	*or*	☐ _____
Buy a used car from?	☐ O.J.	*or*	☐ _____
Hire as a babysitter?	☐ Paris Hilton	*or*	☐ _____
Owe money to?	☐ Al Capone	*or*	☐ _____
Eat for breakfast for a month?	☐ *Fugu* (blowfish)	*or*	☐ _____
_____?	☐ Tonya Harding	*or*	☐ Lil' Kim
_____?	☐ Mastodon	*or*	☐ Mr. Ed
_____?	☐ Jesse James	*or*	☐ Jim Bakker
_____?	☐ Wal-Mart	*or*	☐ The Great Wall of China
_____?	☐ McRib	*or*	☐ McLobster
_____?	☐ Root canal	*or*	☐ Rodeo riding
_____?	☐ Nitroglycerine	*or*	☐ Land mine

217

SOURCES

PART 1: DANGEROUS PEOPLE

Who would you rather have as your barber, Genghis Khan or Attila the Hun?
"Genghis Khan," (2006), Encyclopædia Britannica Online.
"Atilla the Hun," Wikipedia. http://en.wikipedia.org/wiki/Attila_the_
    Hun.
"Attila," (2006), Encyclopædia Britannica Online.

Who would you rather have as a high-school principal, Mao or McCarthy?
"Mao Zedong," The Columbia Electronic Encyclopedia. http://www
    .infoplease.com/ce6/people/A0831663.html.
Biographical Directory of the United States Congress. http://bioguide
    .congress.gov/scripts/biodisplay.pl?index-M000315.
"Joseph McCarthy," Reference.com. http://www.reference.com/browse/
    wiki/Joseph_McCarthy.

Who would you rather have as a high-school football coach, Napoleon or Nixon?
"Napoleon I," (2006), Encyclopædia Britannica Online.
"Nixon, Richard M," (2006), Encyclopædia Britannica Online.
Kilpatrick, Carroll, "Nixon Resigns," *The Washington Post*, August 9, 1974.

Who would you rather have your daughter marry, Hitler or Hussein?
"Adolf Hitler," BBC Online. http://www.bbc.co.uk/history/historic_figures/
hitler_adolf.shtml.

Who would you rather jilt, Lorena Bobbitt or Lizzie Borden?
Labaton, Stephen, "Husband Acquitted of Assault in Mutilation Case," *The
New York Times*, November 11, 1993.
"Tearful Woman Tells Jury Why She Cut Off Her Husband's Penis," *The New
York Times*, November 9, 1993.
Aiuto, Russell, "Lizzie Borden Took An Axe," CourtTV Crime Library. http://
www.crimelibrary.com/notorious_murders/famous/borden/index_
1.html.
Wolf, Buck, "John Wayne Bobbitt Remarries," ABCNews.com. http://
abcnews.go.com/Entertainment/WolfFiles/story?id=91767&page=1.

*Who would you rather have over for a steak dinner, Charles Manson or Jeffrey
Dahmer?*
"The Manson Trial: A Chronology." http://www.law.umkc.edu/faculty/
projects/ftrials/manson/mansonchrono.html.
"Death In Milwaukee," *The New York Times*, July 28, 1991.
Barron, James with Tabor, Mary B. W., "17 Killed, and a Life Is Searched for
Clues," *The New York Times*, August 4, 1991.
"The Biography Channel: Charles Manson." http://www.thebiographychannel
.co.uk/biography_story/306:157/1/Charles_Manson.htm.
"The History of Chocolate." http://www.mce.k12tn.net/chocolate/history/
history_of_chocolate5.htm.

*Who would you rather perform at your son's bar mitzvah, Ozzy Osbourne or
Marilyn Manson?*
"Ozzy Osbourne Biography." http://www.answers.com/topic/ozzy-osbourne.
"Ozzy Osbourne Official Biography." http://www.ozzynet.com.
"The Ozzy FAQ." http://www.faqs.org/faqs/music/ozzy-osbourne-faq.
The Canadian Press Association. September 26, 1984, as quoted in the Ozzy
FAQ.
"Ozzy Osbourne Trivia." http://www.tv.com/ozzy-osbourne/person/2444/
trivia.html.
"Marilyn Manson biography." http://www.starpulse.com/Music/Manson,_
Marilyn/Biography/.

Who would you rather listen to nonstop on a fifteen-hour road trip, Barry Manilow or Neil Diamond?

"Barry Manilow Official Biography." http://www.manilow.com/content/bio .htm.

"Barry Manilow Biography." http://www.vh1.com/artists/az/manilow_ barry/bio.jhtml.

Cooke, Rachel, "Another Sad Lament." *The Observer* (UK), April 9, 2006. http://observer.guardian.co.uk/review/story/0,,1749779,00.html.

"I Am . . . I Said, A Fan of Neil Diamond." http://www.iaisnd.com/ biography.cfm.

"The Biography Channel UK: Neil Diamond Biography." http://www.the biographychannel.co.uk/biography_story/804:627/1/Neil_Diamond .htm.

PART 2: CRITICAL CONDITIONS

Which would be worse to notice on your dentist's hand, flesh-eating bacteria or leprosy?

"Necrotizing Fasciitis," WebMD. http://www.webmd.com/hw/infection/ hw140408.asp?pagenumber=4,

"Leprosy," World Health Organization. http://www.who.int/mediacentre/ factsheets/fs101/en/.

Which would you rather discover in your salad, poison ivy or mistletoe?

Piven, Joshua, et al., "How To Deal With Poison Ivy," *The Worst-Case Scenario Survival Handbook: Golf,* Chronicle Books, 2001.

"Outsmarting Poison Ivy and Its Cousins." http://www.fda.gov/fdac/ features/796_ivy.html.

"Poison Ivy," Savannah River Research Laboratory, University of Georgia. http://www.uga.edu/srel/poison_ivy.htm.

"Mistletoe," Medline Plus Medical Encyclopedia. http://www.nlm.nih.gov/ medlineplus/ency/article/002883.htm.

Shea, Andrea Brewer and Duhl, David, "Myths and Lore of Mistletoe," *The Tennessee Conservationist,* November/December 1997. http://www .state.tn.us/environment/tn_consv/archive/mistltoe.htm.

Piven, Joshua, et al. *The Worst-Case Scenario Survival Handbook: Holidays,* Chronicle Books, 2000.

"True or False: Is Mistletoe the 'Kiss of Death?'" eNature.com. http://www
.enature.com/articles/detail.asp.

Grand, Larry F., "Wild Mushrooms and Poisoning," North Carolina State
University Plant Pathology Extension. http://www.ces.ncsu.edu/depts/
pp/notes/General_Principles/gpin004/gpin004.htm.

*Which would you rather release accidentally by knocking over a vial on a class
trip, black plague or Spanish flu?*

Velendzas, Demetres, "Plague," eMedicine.com. http://www.emedicine
.com/emerg/topic428.htm.

"The Black Death, 1348," EyeWitness to History. http://www.eyewitness
tohistory.com/plague.htm.

"Flu," Centers for Disease Control. http://www.cdc.gov/flu/keyfacts.htm.

Billings, Molly, "The 1918 Influenza Pandemic," Stanford University, http://
virus.stanford.edu/uda/.

"The Influenza of 1918 and the U.S. Navy," Navy Historical Center, Dept. of the
Navy. http://www.history.navy.mil/library/online/influenza_main.htm.

Which would be worse to notice on your date, smallpox or a small handgun?

"Smallpox Overview," Centers for Disease Control. http://www.bt.cdc.gov/
agent/smallpox/overview/disease-facts.asp.

"Population," U.S. Census via FactMonster. http://www.factmonster.com/
ipka/A0004925.html.

"NRA-ILA Factsheet." http://www.nraila.org/Issues/FactSheets/Read
.aspx?ID=83.

"The Brady Campaign Firearm Facts." http://www.bradycampaign.org/
facts/factsheets/pdf/firearm_facts.pdf.

*Which would you rather discover just before an important job interview, a boil
or a goiter?*

"Furuncle," Medline Plus Medical Encyclopedia. http://www.nlm.nih.gov/
medlineplus/ency/article/001474.htm#Symptoms.

"Boils/Skin Abscesses," MedicineNet. http://www.medicinenet.com/boils/
page2.htm.

"Understanding Goiter," WebMD. http://www.webmd.com/content/
article/7/1680_53845.htm.

"Goiter," Medline Plus Medical Encyclopedia. http://www.nlm.nih.gov/
medlineplus/ency/article/001178.htm.

"Goiter," Wikipedia. http://en.wikipedia.org/wiki/Goiter.

"Boil," Wikipedia. http://en.wikipedia.org/wiki/Boil.

Which job would be worse, building the pyramids or building the Panama Canal?

Shaw, Jonathan, "Who Built the Pyramids?" *Harvard Magazine*, July/ August 2003. http://www.harvardmagazine.com/on-line/070391.html.

"Who Built the Pyramids?" NOVAOnline. http://www.pbs.org/wgbh/nova/ pyramid/explore/builders.html.

"Panama Canal," Reference.com. http://www.reference.com/browse/wiki/ Panama_Canal.

"American Canal Construction," Panama Canal History. http://www .pancanal.com/eng/history/history/american.html.

Which would you rather discover in your suburban housing development, Ebola or asbestos?

"Ebola Hemorrhagic Fever," MedlinePlus. http://www.nlm.nih.gov/ medlineplus/ency/article/001339.htm.

"Asbestos, General Information," Environmental Protection Agency. http:// www.epa.gov/asbestos/pubs/help.html#Info.

"Asbestos: What Is It," EPA. http://www.epa.gov/asbestos/pubs/asbe.pdf.

"Where Can Asbestos Be Found?" EPA. http://www.epa.gov/asbestos/pubs/ asbuses.pdf.

"Asbestos-Contaminated Vermiculite," EPA. http://www.epa.gov/asbestos/ pubs/vermfacts.pdf.

"The Scope of the Asbestos Litigation Problem," The Asbestos Alliance. http://asbestossolution.org/scope.html.

Which would be worse, an appendicitis or an audit?

"Appendicitis," National Institutes of Health. http://digestive.niddk.nih .gov/ddiseases/pubs/appendicitis/index.htm.

"Audit, IRS, and Tax," WebTax.com. http://www.wwwebtax.com/audits/ audit_avoiding.htm.

"Appendicitis Facts & Statistics," PR Newswire. http://www.prnewswire .com/mnr/tyco/22115/docs/Appendicitis_Fact_Sheet_FINAL.doc.

Which would be worse, being a gladiator or being a grave robber?

Coleman, Kathleen, "Gladiators: Heroes of the Roman Amphitheatre," BBC On- line. http://www.bbc.co.uk/history/ancient/romans/gladiators_01.shtml.

"Gladiator," Wikipedia. http://en.wikipedia.org/wiki/Gladiator.

"Grave Robber," Wikipedia. http://en.wikipedia.org/wiki/Grave_robber.

"William Burke & William Hare," Crime Library. http://www.crimelibrary
.com/serial_killers/weird/burke/index_1.html.

PART 3: ARCHVILLAINS

Who would you rather face in a dark alley, T. rex or Mike Tyson?

"UCMP Tyrannosaurus rex display information," University of California,
Berkeley. http://www.ucmp.berkeley.edu/museum/public/rexmount
.html.

"Northern State University Guide To Natural Resources." http://www
.northern.edu/natsource/earth/T-rex1.htm.

"T. rex—Warrior or Wimp," BBC Online. http://www.bbc.co.uk/science/
horizon/2004/trexqa.shtml.

Para, Murali, "Iron Mike Tyson: His Place In History," EastSideBoxing.com.
http://www.eastsideboxing.com/news/para2509.php.

"Mike Tyson," Wikipedia. http://en.wikipedia.org/wiki/Mike_Tyson.

Who would you rather have running your blood drive, Werewolf or Dracula?

"Lycaon," Wikipedia. http://en.wikipedia.org/wiki/Lycaon_%28mythology
%29.

"Werewolf," Wikipedia. http://en.wikipedia.org/wiki/Werewolf.

"Werewolf," Encyclopedia Mythica. http://www.pantheon.org/articles/w/
werewolf.html.

"Count Dracula's Legend," RomaniaTourism.com. http://www.romania
tourism.com/dracula.html.

Who would you rather have as the IT guy, the Terminator or HAL 9000?

"Trivia for *The Terminator* (1984)," Internet Movie Database. http://www
.imdb.com/title/tt0088247/trivia.

"HAL 9000," Wikipedia. http://en.wikipedia.org/wiki/HAL_9000.

"Skynet," Wikipedia. http://en.wikipedia.org/wiki/Skynet.

Who would you rather have as a father, Darth Vader or Don Corleone?

"Godfather Quotes," Internet Movie Database. http://www.imdb.com/title/
tt0068646/quotes.

"Trivia for *The Godfather*," Internet Movie Database. http://www.imdb.com/title/tt0068646/trivia.

"AFI's 100 Years . . . 100 Heroes and Villains," American Film Institute. http://www.afi.com/tvevents/100years/handv.aspx.

Who would you rather have as a high-school chemistry teacher, Alien or Predator?

"Predator (film)," Wikipedia. http://en.wikipedia.org/wiki/Predator_(film).

"Alien," Answers.com. http://www.answers.com/topic/alien-movie-1979.

Who would you rather have catering your party, Neanderthals or ninjas?

"Neanderthal Man," Columbia Encyclopedia, Sixth Edition. http://www.bartleby.com/65/nn/Nndrtlmn.html.

"Japanese Arts: History, Ninja History," The Shaolin Society. http://www.shaolin-society.co.uk/shaolin_legacy/history.php?history=10.

"Neanderthal," Wikipedia. http://en.wikipedia.org/wiki/Neanderthal.

PART 4: KILLER CREATURES

Which would you rather discover in your backyard, a West Nile mosquito or a West African dictator?

"West Nile Virus, What You Need To Know," Centers for Disease Control. http://www.cdc.gov/ncidod/dvbid/westnile/wnv_factsheet.html and http://www.atsdr.cdc.gov/consultations/west_nile_virus/index.html.

"Charles Taylor, preacher, warlord and president," BBC Online. http://news.bbc.co.uk/1/hi/world/africa/2963086.stm.

"Charles Taylor, A wanted man," CNN.com. http://www.cnn.com/2003/WORLD/africa/06/10/liberia.taylor/index.html.

"Charles Taylor," Wikipedia. http://en.wikipedia.org/wiki/Charles_G._Taylor.

"How Mosquitoes Work," HowStuffWorks.com. http://science.howstuffworks.com/mosquito.htm.

Which would be worse to find in your slipper, a black widow or a giant centipede?

Jones, Susan C., "Black Widow Spider, HYG-2061A-04," Ohio State University Fact Sheet. http://ohioline.osu.edu/hyg-fact/2000/2061A.html.

"Giant Centipede," St. Louis Zoo. http://www.stlzoo.org/animals/about theanimals/invertebrates/centipedes/giantcentipede.htm.

Which would you rather notice swimming below your inner tube, a barracuda or a Portuguese man-of-war?

"Planet Ocean: Barracuda," Discovery School.com. http://school.discovery .com/schooladventures/planetocean/barracuda.html.

"Great Barracuda," Florida Museum of Natural History Ichthyology Department. http://www.flmnh.ufl.edu/fish/Gallery/Descript/Great Barracuda/GreatBarracuda.html.

"Portuguese Man-of-War," National Geographic. http://www3.national geographic.com/animals/invertebrates/portuguese-man-of-war .html.

"Poisonous Plants and Animals: Blue bottle," ThinkQuest. http://library .thinkquest.org/C007974/2_1bbo.htm.

Which would be more deadly once per week, a pack of wolves or a pack of cigarettes?

"Gray Wolf," U.S. Fish and Wildlife Service. http://www.fws.gov/species/ species_accounts/bio_gwol.html.

"Wolf Park General Wolf Information Page," Wolf Park. http://www .wolfpark.org/wolffaq.html.

"The Heath Consequences of Smoking," A Report of the Surgeon General, Centers for Disease Control. http://www.cdc.gov/Tobacco/sgr/sgr_ 2004/Factsheets/10.htm.

Which would be worse to spot just outside your pup tent, rats or Rambo?

"Brown rat," BBC Science and Nature Wildfacts. http://www.bbc.co.uk/ nature/wildfacts/factfiles/273.shtml.

"Brown Rat," Wikipedia. http://en.wikipedia.org/wiki/Brown_Rat.

"Rat Fact Sheet," Illinois Department of Public Health. http://www.idph .state.il.us/envhealth/pcnorwayrat.htm.

"Rambo: First Blood Part II," Wikipedia. http://en.wikipedia.org/wiki/ Rambo:_First_Blood_Part_II.

"Rambo," Wikipedia. http://en.wikipedia.org/wiki/John_Rambo.

"First Blood" (1982), Internet Movie Database. http://www.imdb.com/title/ tt0083944/.

Which would be worse to wake up to, vampire bats or hookworms?

"Vampire Bats: Animal Information," National Geographic. http://www
.nationalgeographic.com/kids/creature_feature/0110/bats2.html.

"Unlike other bats, vampire bats keep out of trouble by running, Cornell re-
searchers find," Cornell University News Service. http://www.news
.cornell.edu/stories/March05/Riskin.bats.snd.html.

"Vampire Bats," Wikipedia. http://en.wikipedia.org/wiki/Vampire_bat.

"Hookworm Fact Sheet," Division of Parasitic Diseases, Centers for Disease
Control. http://www.cdc.gov/ncidod/dpd/parasites/hookworm/factsht_
hookworm.htm.

Haburchak, David R., "Hookworms," eMedicine.com, http://www
.emedicine.com/med/topic1028.htm.

Which would you rather have as a house pet, Jaws or Godzilla?

"Pet Sharks," Aquatic Community. http://www.aquaticcommunity.com/
universal-viewid233.html.

"Godzilla," Wikipedia. http://en.wikipedia.org/wiki/Godzilla.

*Which would you rather have as a breakfast cereal, harvester ants or rattle-
snakes?*

Nickerson, J. C., "Florida Harvester Ant," Florida Department of Agriculture
and Consumer Services, Division of Plant Industry. http://creatures
.ifas.ufl.edu/urban/ants/harvester_ant.htm.

Drees, Bastiaan M., "Red Harvester Ants," Texas A&M University Agricultural Extension Service. http://insects.tamu.edu/extension/bulletins/
l-5314.html.

"How Dangerous Are Rattlesnakes?" American International Rattlesnake
Museum. http://www.rattlesnakes.com/core.html.

"Rattlesnakes," Wikipedia. http://en.wikipedia.org/wiki/Rattlesnake.

PART 5: PERILOUS PLACES

Which would be worse, chopping onions or making sausage?

"Boudin Noir," Hertzmann.com. http://www.hertzmann.com/articles/2002/
boudin/.

"Haggis," GumboPages.com. http://www.gumbopages.com/food/scottish/
haggis.html.

Which would be worse, lunch at Neverland Ranch or breakfast at a poultry-processing plant?

"Star's Home Was 'Pleasure Island,'" BBC Online. http://news.bbc.co.uk/2/hi/entertainment/4359809.stm.

"Neverland Ranch," Wikipedia. http://en.wikipedia.org/wiki/Neverland_Ranch.

"Jackson pays back wages, closes Neverland estate," *The Washington Times*, March 16, 2006. http://www.washtimes.com/national/20060318-112957-3070r.htm.

"OSHA's New DRAFT Ergonomics Guidelines for Poultry Processing," OSHA. http://www.osha.gov/pls/oshaweb/owadisp.show_document?p_table=SPEECHES&p_id=727.

"Injury and Injustice—America's Poultry Industry," United Food and Commercial Workers. http://www.ufcw.org/press_room/fact_sheets_and_backgrounder/poultryindustry_.cfm.

"OSHA Hazard Information Bulletins: Contracting Occupationally Related Psittacosis," OSHA. http://www.osha.gov/dts/hib/hib_data/hib19940808.html.

Which would be worse, visiting North Korea with Geraldo Rivera or getting trapped among the Donners with Joan Rivers?

"Geraldo Rivera," Wikipedia. http://en.wikipedia.org/wiki/Geraldo_Rivera.

Carr, David, "Pentagon Says Geraldo Will Be Removed From Iraq," *The New York Times*, April 1, 2003.

"Joan Rivers Biography." http://www.joanrivers.com/AllAboutJoan/Joan_Rivers_Bio06.pdf.

"PETA: Joan Rivers Touts the 'Ham That Even Jews Can Eat' for Passover," PETA. http://www.peta.org/feat/JoanRivers/.

"Joan Rivers," Wikipedia. http://en.wikipedia.org/wiki/Joan_Rivers.

"American Experience, The Donner Party," PBS. http://www.pbs.org/wgbh/amex/donner/filmmore/fd.html.

Which would be worse, a cruise on the Love Boat to Krakatoa or the running of the bulls in Pamplona handcuffed to Frank Sinatra?

"Krakatau, Indonesia (1883)," San Diego State University Department of Geology. http://www.geology.sdsu.edu/how_volcanoes_work/Krakatau.html.

"Krakatoa," Wikipedia. http://en.wikipedia.org/wiki/Krakatoa.

"The Love Boat," Wikipedia. http://en.wikipedia.org/wiki/The_Love_Boat.

"The Love Boat (1977)," Internet Movie Database. http://www.imdb.com/title/tt0075529/.

"Google Music: Frank Sinatra," Google.com. http://www.google.com/musicad?aid=8vN74lv6LHK.

Which would be worse, initiation night at the Hells Angels book club or flight training at kamikaze pilot school?

Thompson, Hunter S., "The Motorcycle Gangs," *The Nation*, May 17, 1965. http://www.thenation.com/doc/19650517/thompson.

"Hells Angels: History," Hells Angels Motorcycle Club. http://www.hells-angels.com/history.htm.

Sasaki, Mako "Who Became Kamikaze Pilots and How Did They Feel about Their Mission?", *The Concord Review*, 1997. http://www.tcr.org/tcr/essays/EPrize_Kamikaze.pdf.

"Kamikaze," Wikipedia. http://en.wikipedia.org/wiki/Kamikaze.

Which would be worse, wine tasting during trench warfare or party planning with George Armstrong Custer?

"How to serve wine." Wine Online. http://www.wineonline.ie/kitchen/serving.htm.

"Wine Definitions: Acrid to Zesty," Tasting-Wine.com. http://www.tasting-wine.com/html/wine-terms.html.

Duffy, Michael, "Life in the Trenches," First World War.com. http://www.firstworldwar.com/features/trenchlife.htm.

"PBS: The West, George Armstrong Custer," PBS. http://www.pbs.org/weta/thewest/people/a_c/custer.htm.

"Battle of Little Bighorn," Wikipedia. http://en.wikipedia.org/wiki/Battle_of_the_Little_Bighorn.

Which would be worse, ten hours in Baghdad or ten hours in Baltimore?

Tavernise, Sabrina, et al., "Iraqi Dead May Total 600,000," *The New York Times*, October 10, 2006. http://www.nytimes.com/2006/10/11/world/middleeast/11casualties.html.

"The Real Cost of the Iraq War to American Taxpayers," The Democratic Party. http://www.democrats.org/a/p/the_real_cost_of_the_iraq_war_to_american_taxpayers.html.

"Crime Rate Comparison: Baltimore vs. Detroit," areaConnect.com. http://

baltimore.areaconnect.com/crime/compare.htm?c1=Baltimore=MD& c2=Detroit&s2=MI.

Ditkoff, Anna, "Murder by Numbers, A Look Behind the Sad Statistics Of Baltimore's 2005 Homicide Toll," *Baltimore City Paper*, Jan 18, 2006. http://www.citypaper.com/news/story.asp?id=11352.

"Exile Gun Felons," Editorial, *The Baltimore Sun*, October 16, 2006.

Eldridge, Earle, "In Baltimore, We're Waiting," *The Examiner*, Oct 16, 2006. http://www.examiner.com/a-345600~In_Baltimore__we_re_waiting .html.

Dechter, Gadi and Donovan, "Doug, Mayor Defends Grading Change," *The Baltimore Sun*, August 16, 2006. http://www.baltimoresun.com/news/ education/bal-md.schools16aug16001518,0,2434135.story?coll=bal-education-utility.

ABOUT THE AUTHOR

Josh Piven is bad, but he used to be worse. He's the author of more than a dozen nonfiction and humor books, including *The Escape Artists* and *The Worst-Case Scenario Survival Handbook*. He and his obliging family live in Philadelphia. Visit www.josh piven.net for excerpts of new books and cool stuff that can only be experienced with a computer.